trees &
shrubs

JimHole LoisHole

questions & ANSWERS

volume 5

trees &
shrubs

Practical Advice and the
Science Behind It

H|
HOLE'S
ENJOY GARDENING

Published by Hole's
101 Bellerose Drive
St. Albert, Alberta Canada
T8N 8N8

Copyright © Hole's 2001

Printed in Canada   5   4   3   2   1

National Library of Canada Cataloguing in Publication Data

Hole, Jim, 1956–
   Trees and shrubs

   (Questions and answers ; 5)
   Includes index.
   ISBN 0-9682791-9-8

   1. Ornamental trees--Miscellanea. 2. Ornamental shrubs--Miscellanea.
I. Hole, Lois, 1933- II. Title. III. Series: Questions & answers (St. Albert,
Alta.) ; 5.

SB435.H65 2001   635.9'76   C00-911651-6

Colour separations and film by Elite Lithographers, Edmonton, Alberta, Canada
Printed and bound by Quality Color Press, Edmonton, Alberta, Canada

Contents

Acknowledgements

Thanks to the staff of our Trees and Shrubs department, especially Christina McDonald and nursery manager Shane Neufeld, for their continuing enthusiasm and insightful assistance. We'd also like to thank our other staff members, particularly the staff in our new call centre, who often fielded hundreds of calls per day and still found time to record questions used for this book.

Thanks also to those people who sent questions by e-mail at *yourquestions@enjoygardening.com*. Keep them coming!

Finally, thanks to Mr. Atkinson, the English immigrant who, so many years ago, shared his love of trees with everyone in the community. His passion encouraged us to plant saplings, which have grown into tall, proud, strong trees that provide life-enriching beauty and shelter every day. We hope they will endure for decades to come.

The Q&A Series

Practical Advice and the Science Behind It

Trees & Shrubs: Practical Advice and the Science Behind It completes the first phase of our Q&A project. With the major gardening topics covered— bedding plants, roses, perennials, vegetables, and trees and shrubs—we look forward to turning our attention to more-specialized gardening pursuits. Future Q&A books will focus on alpine gardens, landscaping, fruits, bulbs, and indoor plants. We're even considering a Q&A on backyard barbecuing! The possibilities are as limitless as your questions, which have provided the inspiration for this series.

Trees & Shrubs has been our most demanding volume so far. When we were compiling answers for the book, we often ran into questions like this one: "I have a small pine that was specially imported for my garden. I've been very careful with it, but it's losing needles and turning brown. What can I do?" There are so many potential reasons for this pine's condition that it would take an entire chapter to explore them all fully—and without actually observing the tree, it would be impossible to know which possible answer was actually the right one! Thus, you may find that you have new questions after you read our answers—and we think that's just great!

Success is built on a solid foundation of questions. Every innovation comes about because someone wondered, "How does this process work? And how can I make it work better?" A good question can open up whole new worlds—new ways of doing things, new perspectives, and new information about secrets once hidden.

That information is what good gardening is all about. Our goal has always been to provide gardeners, no matter what their skill level, with the information they need to grow beautiful plants—and to accomplish this in the most enjoyable manner possible. Accordingly, different people want different kinds of information. In this book we've answered questions in two parts: a short answer for those who are eager to solve a problem and get back to their projects, and a more in-depth answer for those who want to spend a little time learning what makes their favourite hobby work. In short, we deliver practical advice and the science behind it.

Answering these questions has been as valuable for us as it has for the questioners. They've pushed us to the limits of our knowledge, urging us to dig deeper for the truth.

Lois Hole and Jim Hole
March 2001

Introduction
By Jim Hole

When my brother Bill and I were in the second and first grade, respectively, Mom and Dad took us out to the front yard of our farmhouse and helped us plant two spruce trees. The trees were only about six inches tall, and I remember wondering how such tiny plants could possibly survive the first winter. But they did survive, and as I watched them grow over the years, I learned firsthand just how tenacious woody plants are.

The durability of trees and shrubs, along with their great beauty, has inspired in me a passion that is shared by many. Old trees often evoke powerful images of our past, images as sharp as the pictures in a photo album.

The Big Maple Tree

Whenever I touch the majestic maple tree in Mom and Dad's yard, I recall the storm twenty-five years ago that split it down the middle. This was the tree that my friends and I had spent hours climbing as kids, so I couldn't just let it die. I drilled a hole through the tree and inserted a long, threaded metal rod. A washer and nut on each end held the trunk together, and eventually the breach healed. That tree is still hale and hearty today, and if you look closely, you can still see the old, rusted remains of my teenage repair job.

That my improvised repair job actually worked was quite a learning experience, and I also learned a lot from helping Mom and Dad care for the shelter belt they'd planted to protect the farm. Over the years I watered, fertilized, and pruned hundreds of willows, spruce, and poplars, becoming familiar with their likes and dislikes.

That knowledge came in handy when Mom and Dad started selling a few trees and shrubs in the early 1970s, when we still had our market-gardening operation. A decade later, trees and shrubs would play a much larger role in our business.

Branching Out

In 1982, after successful forays into market gardening and commercial vegetable production, the family decided to get into the retail garden centre business. Although our main focus at that time was bedding plants, we did our best to cover most of the gardening bases, and so, we included trees and shrubs in our inventory. This "nursery" was a pretty humble affair, just a few dozen square feet of gravel and concrete located in between the growing range and the garden centre. But the trees and shrubs proved popular enough to justify the creation of a permanent nursery, so we made a space for one alongside the garden centre.

Not long after we took this step, we hired a young man named Shane Neufeld to work in the nursery. It wasn't too long before he became our nursery manager, and his extensive knowledge and deep love for trees and shrubs have proved invaluable. We began with about 100 varieties of trees and shrubs; today, Shane regularly orders over 600 varieties of shade trees, evergreens, and shrubs. That diversity is reflected in the questions we receive, which have grown in number as steadily as our stock.

Deep-Rooted Passions

Some of those questions reveal just how much emotion people invest in trees, as well as a deep curiosity about how they grow. Once a man called me to settle a bet; he put me on a speakerphone so that a half-dozen or so of his giggling friends could hear my answer . "Are there male and female trees?' the man asked in a tone that suggested he knew what the answer was going to be. "Well, yes, there are," I said, and instantly I heard the man making sounds of disgust—that wasn't the response he'd expected. There was a hearty round of laughter from his friends, and more than one cry of "I told you so!"

Several years ago, we received a visit from an infuriated wife who seemed on the verge of divorcing her husband. It seems that he'd found some caterpillars in their trees and figured that a good dose of chemicals would solve the problem. Well, he was right, after a fashion; the chemical he chose was a herbicide that got rid of the bugs all right, but only because it killed all of the trees in the yard, thereby starving the insects to death. How does that saying go, about the cure being worse than the disease? The only advice we could give the poor woman was to direct her to a certified arborist who could properly dispose of her dead trees.

Thankfully, such horror stories are the exception, not the rule, when people ask me about trees and shrubs. Far more often they'll be looking for simple advice on pruning or watering. In the end, all tree lovers share the same desire: to enjoy them for as long as possible, and perhaps even to leave them behind as a legacy.

The Shape of Things to Come

Today, over thirty-five years later, the pair of spruce Bill and I planted tower above our old farmhouse. They've stood firm and proud for so long that they almost feel like family members. That's the magic of trees: their venerability lends them a mythic power that other plants can't match. As the spruce have grown, so has our knowledge and passion for trees. But there's still plenty of growth to come; those spruce could enjoy another century of life. While I doubt I'll be around that long, I do know that people will continue to learn about trees and shrubs, and in so doing we will discover how best to live with and enjoy these remarkable plants.

The Structure of Tree & Shrub Gardening

Mom and I see trees and shrubs differently. While we both appreciate their beauty, Mom tends to take a practical approach when it comes to caring for them. She's content to water and fertilize them, while I like to watch for pest problems and handle the pruning. Similarly, Mom has a better eye for subtle colours and textures, while I derive satisfaction from learning about the inner lives of trees. Together, I think we cover almost all of the topics that interest other tree and shrub lovers. And if there's a question we can't answer, we turn to our tree and shrub experts, nursery manager Shane Neufeld and his assistant Christina McDonald. Shane and Christina were instrumental in the production of this book.

Trees & Shrubs: Practical Advice and the Science Behind It is divided into six sections that cover the most important fundamentals of planting and caring for trees and shrubs.

The Basics

Once established, trees and shrubs tend to look after themselves quite well. You may have to water during a dry spell or prune if limbs start getting tangled or unstable, but by and large, these sturdy plants can fend for themselves. Still, there are some critical points to remember when establishing trees and shrubs in their new homes. Here's one: like any other plant, trees and shrubs must be planted in the right soil to thrive. A soil rich in organic matter is still the best choice for virtually all trees and shrubs, provided that water can still drain freely. Soils that are very alkaline, however, will not accommodate acid-loving shrubs like rhododendrons and azaleas. They are destined to fail unless the soil can be amended.

Choosing Trees & Shrubs

When you purchase a tree or shrub, there's one critical check that you must not forget. For every tree you buy at nursery, there's an ideal ratio between the root ball and the height of the tree. For example, when buying a tall, columnar conifer like a pine, if the height of the tree in the nursery is 100 cm, the diameter of the root ball should be no less than 40 cm. A large root ball indicates that the tree has had enough nutrients to thrive during its time in the nursery. The Canadian Nursery Trades Association has set standards for root ball sizes, so don't be afraid to check the Canadian Standards for Nursery Stock guide before you purchase your tree.

Planting

Choosing the right location for your trees and shrubs is vital, partly because where you plant them can affect your entire garden. A family friend had a fantastic tomato patch that produced heavy yields of large, juicy fruit season after season. But one year, she noticed that the tomatoes were smaller, and the yields were down. She shrugged it off, but the year after that, the problem had gotten a little worse, and the year after that, her yields were poorer still, no matter how much extra water and fertilizer she gave them. The solution struck her one day as she was standing in the tomato patch, under the shade of her elm trees…trees that had finally grown tall enough to drastically reduce the light available to her tomatoes. When you plant trees, you have to plan ahead!

The Growing Season

Patience's ultimate reward must be the satisfaction of having a tree grow up with you. But it's not simply a matter of digging a hole and tossing in a random acorn! To nurture a tree to maturity, you may need to give the seeds special treatment or start from cuttings. Then there's the annual job of pruning, and protecting your plants from winter's chill and hungry rodents and deer. Still, with a little work and a lot of patience, one day you will be able to point out a tall elm or maple and say to a friend, "You know, I planted that tree back in 2001…"

Enjoy Trees & Shrubs

As a kid, my favourite way to enjoy trees was to climb them; now, I like to revel in their size and majesty. And I take great comfort in the natural forms and scents of shrubs. But for those of you who enjoy taking some cuttings for a vase on the kitchen table, by all means do so; there's nothing like the scent of fresh lilacs wafting through the house.

Troubleshooting

Even self-reliant trees and shrubs aren't without their problems. What happens, for example, when you have to move them? Moving trees isn't as simple as taking your perennials along with you when you move from one house to another. Unlike most other plants, mature trees and shrubs are fixtures, even landmarks. At the western end of our greenhouse facilities, we had a huge poplar, around which we'd built the perennial information booth. People loved the fact that the tree grew right through the middle of the booth, but of course that situation couldn't last forever; eventually, the tree outgrew the holes we'd left in the shed. Now, we could have taken the shed apart, but poplars are short-lived trees and this one was well beyond its expected lifespan anyway, so we reluctantly chopped it down. That was a hard choice, but in the end, I think we did the right thing.

Varieties

If I had to choose my favourite tree variety (or, more properly, species), I'd go with maples. There are good reasons the maple leaf is Canada's national symbol: various maple species grow all across the country, and all of these species are tall, strong, and beautiful. But that's only if I were forced to choose; the truth is, I love almost all trees and shrubs. Each has its own charm.

Passion & Pride

Trees inspire gardeners (and even people who don't think of themselves as gardeners) to great heights of altruism. Dutch elm disease has been moving steadily westward and northward since its introduction to the eastern US in the 1930s. The disease has destroyed untold thousands of elm trees, but people aren't giving up without a fight. Many cities across the continent have started information campaigns designed to save their elms, and people are taking these rules to heart. They know not to prune when the fungus-spreading elm bark beetles are active and can easily penetrate the open wounds in freshly cut branches. They don't bring firewood, which can harbour the beetles, into the city after camping trips. They remember to sterilize their pruning equipment. And they keep their eyes open for diseased trees so that they can be removed, which helps inhibit the disease's spread.

Edmonton and its surrounding municipalities remain among the few islands on the continent where Dutch elm disease has yet to find a foothold. Our geographical position helps: elms don't occur naturally in our river valleys, whereas they do in Saskatchewan and Manitoba. Thus, the bark beetles don't have a convenient path of elms to follow into Alberta.

But I think much of our good fortune can be attributed to the high value people place on trees. A huge, healthy tree is a source of spiritual strength for humans. It's no wonder that people go to such lengths to preserve them.

CHAPTER 1 ❧
THE BASICS

A good knowledge of basic growing information is your best foundation for building a yard with vigorous trees and shrubs. Knowing the life span, soil requirements, and even the geographical origin of a plant helps you nurture it properly and avoid potential problems. Besides, it can be fascinating to delve into the history of plants; you never know what amazing stories lurk in their past.

Definitions

What's the difference between trees and shrubs?

Lois ❖ By strict definition, a tree is a tall woody plant with a single trunk supporting a leafy crown. A shrub is a smaller woody plant that naturally branches at ground level. Trees also usually live longer than shrubs.

Jim ❖ Mom's definition is a good general one. But as with everything in life, there are exceptions that fit both categories—the taller lilacs and some maples, for example.

Climate can also change a tree to a shrub. For example, a sugar maple may grow into a tall, stately tree in a mild climate, but it will remain a shrub (due to winterkill) in a climate that is fairly harsh.

What is a standard tree?

Lois ❖ "Standard" describes a tree with a single predominate stem or trunk. But this is not to say that this form is the tree's natural growth habit. Many trees and shrubs are trained and sold as standards although they naturally have a multi-stemmed habit.

Jim ❖ According to the Canadian Standards for Nursery Stock, standard trees should have straight, sturdy trunks with a well-branched and balanced head.

Why aren't trees listed by Latin names the way perennials are?

Lois ❖ Many trees and shrubs are commonly known by their Latin names. For example, *Gingko*, *Magnolia*, *Hydrangea*, *Viburnum*, and *Rhododendron* are all Latin names. Other common names are very close to their Latin counterparts: *Populus* is poplar, *Juniperus* is juniper, and *Spiraea* is spirea. You may have been using Latin names all along and not have known it!

Jim ❖ All plants (and all organisms for that matter) have Latin, or scientific, names. The scientific community relies on Latin names to avoid confusion between species. Common names vary widely from place to place, but Latin names describe only one species.

Sometimes a plant's common name is used more often than its Latin name, or vice versa. A less-familiar plant, a rare perennial, for example, will tend to be known by its Latin name simply because it doesn't have a history of common name use. A tree like the maple, on the other hand, has such an extensive history of common name use that "maple" will almost always be the first descriptor used.

What does "cultivar" mean? What's the difference between a cultivar and a species?

Lois ❖ Cultivar is a shortened form of "cultivated variety." In plain language, this means that the plant variety exists because of human intervention.

Jim ❖ A species is a distinct group of plants that regularly interbreed with each other. A single species may include many different cultivars. Cultivars are a result of breeding work to produce specific desirable characteristics, such as foliage colour and shape, height, hardiness, increased fruit yield, and amount and colour of bloom. For example, the Norway Maple species (*Acer platanoides*) includes such cultivars as 'Crimson King,' 'Harlequin,' and 'Emerald Jade,' all bred for specific characteristics.

What does "caliper" mean when referring to trees?

Jim ❖ Caliper is the diameter of a tree's trunk. This measurement is usually taken about 30 cm above the ground or occasionally at the place where the trunk and root meet at the soil line. Trees are often priced by caliper size; typically, the larger the caliper, the more expensive the tree.

Measuring the caliper of a tree.

What does "field grown" mean?

Jim ❖ Field-grown trees and shrubs are grown in field soil rather than in pots or containers. Whether trees are grown in pots or in the field generally depends on the grower's preference.

What is a whip?

Lois ❖ A whip is a young tree, often without branches. Whips are inexpensive, but of course they take longer to reach maturity than branched nursery stock of the same variety.

What is the crown of a tree?

Lois ❖ The crown is where the tree begins to branch out. Some trees have very pronounced crowns—almost lollipop shaped—while other crowns may be less pronounced. The crown can take many forms, from round to tear-dropped to columnar.

What are codominant trunks?

Jim ❖ Codominant trunks are trunks of equal size that divide, forming a characteristic Y-shaped pattern. Codominant stems are prone to splitting, because the bark doesn't form a strong union at the crotch (the area of the tree where the two branches meet). The simplest cure for codominant stems is to prevent them from forming in the first place. Corrective pruning to one trunk, or terminal, early in the tree's life will eliminate codominant stems.

What's the difference between deciduous and coniferous trees?

Jim ❖ Deciduous trees are leafless for part of the year, usually winter. They may also be called broad-leaf trees, referring to the shape of the leaves they produce. Coniferous trees produce cones and usually have fine, needle-like leaves.

What's the difference between conifers and evergreens?

Lois ❖ When we say evergreen, we immediately think of species like spruce and pine. But an evergreen can be any plant that doesn't shed its leaves over the winter. Holly is just one example. Conifers aren't necessarily evergreens. Larch, for example, is a conifer but not an evergreen. It produces cones but sheds its needles in the fall.

'Hillside Creeper' pine

Soil

What type of soil is best for trees and shrubs?

Lois ❖ You must consider the type of tree or shrub you're planting. Different species have different requirements. Birch trees, for instance, prefer a rich, moist, acidic soil, whereas caraganas prefer dry, sandy soil.

Jim ❖ Most trees and shrubs prefer a mineral soil with at least two percent organic matter. "Mineral" refers to the non-organic portion of the soil; in other words, remove all living and dead matter from soil and what's left are minerals. A mineral soil is strong enough to anchor roots, provides good drainage, and offers sufficient moisture- and nutrient-holding capacity for good tree growth.

What is a soil test? Can I do it myself?

Lois ❖ A simple soil test is a standardized method of measuring the nutrients that make up your soil and determining your soil pH. There are also more sophisticated tests that will provide you with micronutrient levels and level of soil salts. These more-detailed tests are generally used by commercial growers. For a home gardener, a basic soil test is usually adequate.

You can perform a reasonably accurate soil pH and nutrient test yourself. Kits are available from most garden centres.

Should I get my soil tested?

Lois ❖ You should get your soil tested if you have a very large yard or acreage or if you have a history of plants growing poorly in a specific area of your garden despite proper care.

Jim ❖ If you have specific problem areas in your garden, it's a good idea to get a soil test. You can learn as much from a soil test as you would from several years of trial and error. If your garden is large or has distinct soil pockets, you may need to perform several tests. Take a core sample 15 cm into the topsoil. Take samples from different spots in your garden and mix them. This way you get a more representative, and more accurate, measure of your garden. The problem with soil tests for trees and shrubs is that there is very little data to suggest what the appropriate levels of soil nutrients actually are.

What does a soil test tell me?

Jim ❖ A basic soil test provides an array of information:

• Levels of the major nutrients: nitrogen (N), phosphate (P), and potash (K). These nutrients are represented by the numbers on a fertilizer label; that is, 10-52-10 means 10 percent nitrogen, 52 percent phosphate, and 10 percent potash. Sulphur levels are also sometimes included.

• pH level: the soil's acidity or basicity.

• Level of soluble salts: plants burn if the concentration is too high.

• Soil texture: the relative quantities of sand, silt, clay, and organic matter.

An advanced soil test may include the levels of the other essential plant nutrients: iron, molybdenum, sulphur, magnesium, calcium, zinc, copper, and boron. Normally, only commercial growers use such tests.

For farmers, it can be very expensive not to test soil. For example, a deficiency of 20 kg of nitrogen per hectare adds up to a 10,000-kg shortage on a 500-hectare farm. That shortfall could result in catastrophic crop-yield losses. Thankfully, the stakes aren't as high for home gardeners. However, if you're having trouble growing healthy plants, it's worth spending a few dollars to test your soil.

Why is my soil's pH important?

Lois ❖ It's all a question of balance. When you have the proper balance of acidity and alkalinity, you meet the needs of both your plants and the organisms in the soil. That's a great step on the way to growing trees and shrubs successfully!

Jim ❖ Let's review our chemistry. pH is a scale for measuring acids and bases. On this scale, 7.0 is neutral—neither acidic nor alkaline. (Pure water is normally pH 7.0.) As the numbers go down (6.9, 6.8, etc.), the acidity increases. As the numbers rise (7.1, 7.2, etc.), the alkalinity increases.

In alkaline soil, many essential nutrients remain bound up as insoluble compounds. That means your trees and shrubs have a harder time absorbing nutrients from the soil. For example, in many prairie regions, high pH causes foliage to become "veiny" or deficient in iron.

However, when the pH is too low, plants tend to absorb excessive quantities of trace elements, particularly metals like iron and zinc, which can be toxic. As well, many beneficial soil micro-organisms, which convert elements like nitrogen into forms that plants can use, cannot survive in very acidic soils.

How do I adjust my soil's pH?

Lois ❖ Assuming you have tested your soil's pH, take the results to a good garden centre. A staff member should be able to give you reliable advice on which amendments to add to improve your soil's pH.

Jim ❖ To adjust the pH, you must amend your soil. Sulphur lowers your soil's pH (making it more acidic) while horticultural lime raises the pH (making it more alkaline). You can purchase these products at most garden centres.

If you're adding sulphur, stick with very fine sulphur or aluminum sulphate: coarse sulphur reacts too slowly to benefit your trees and shrubs. If you're adding lime, use dolomitic lime, because it contains both calcium and magnesium (two important plant nutrients). Be sure to buy a fine grade of lime that will react quickly in the soil.

How much sulphur/lime to add to soil to change pH levels

GARDEN SULPHUR* kg/100 m² (to lower pH)

Desired pH Change	Sands	Loam	Clay
8.5–6.5	23	29	34
8.0–6.5	14	17	23
7.5–6.5	6	9	12
7.0–6.5	1	2	3

* although sulphur is effective, it is slow to react in soil

LIMESTONE kg/100 m² (to increase pH)

Desired pH Change	Sandy loam	Loam	Silt Loam	Clay
4.0–6.5	58	80	97	115
4.5–6.5	48	67	97	115
5.0–6.5	39	53	64	76
5.5–6.5	30	39	46	53
6.0–6.5	16	22	25	28

columnar aspen

How does compost improve my soil?

Lois ❖ Compost adds necessary nutrients and beneficial soil micro-organisms. It replaces lost organic matter and loosens the soil for root penetration. Compost also reduces erosion.

Jim ❖ Compost serves a couple other purposes as well. It acts as a wonderful mulch to reduce weeds and maintain soil moisture, and it diverts valuable organic material from landfills. Composting makes good sense.

Why is good drainage important?

Lois ❖ If you don't have adequate drainage, your trees and shrubs will literally drown. It's as simple as that.

Jim ❖ We often think that water is the only critical soil factor for proper tree growth, but oxygen is just as important. Poorly drained soils trap water, starving plants' roots for oxygen. In order for roots to breathe, the soil must be porous enough that air can infiltrate easily. When the concentration of air drops below about three percent of the soil volume, root growth stops.

Many beneficial soil organisms can't survive in waterlogged soils. Various bacteria and fungi in the soil break down organic matter into nutrients for your trees and shrubs to absorb. Without these nutrients, the plants eventually starve.

How do I check whether my soil has proper drainage?

Lois ❖ If your soil has proper drainage, water won't stay on its surface for long. It will be absorbed quickly—you can watch it disappear into the soil in just a few minutes.

Oddly enough, the signs of overwatering (poor drainage) and underwatering trees and shrubs are similar: yellowing of foliage, limp stems and branches, and leaf drop.

Jim ❖ Dig a hole 20–30 cm deep, fill it with water, and watch. The water should drain away slowly but steadily, leaving the hole empty within an hour. If the water just sits, the drainage is poor. Work in plenty of organic matter to improve soil drainage. On the other hand, if the water drains out of the hole almost immediately, you have excessively porous or sandy soil. This won't necessarily harm your plants, but it does mean you'll have to water and fertilize more frequently.

Some certified arborists use a device called a penetrometer to check soil drainage. It measures compaction based on the resistance exerted on the tool when it is pushed into the ground.

Can I fix soil that drains too quickly?

Lois ❖ Yes. The best solution is to add organic matter, for example, well-rotted manure, compost, or peat moss.

Jim ❖ Regularly adding organic matter to the soil will help you strike the right balance between drainage and water retention. Organic material causes the clay particles to flocculate (stick together) into larger, distinct particles. Good soil has a blocky structure, and small blocks allow roots and air to penetrate the soil more easily. Organic matter also helps to hold water in the soil.

Life cycles

How long do trees live?

Lois ❖ You can expect trees or shrubs with short lifespans to live less than 50 years. Trees with average lifespans will live about 50 to 100 years. A tree with a long lifespan should still be going strong at 100 years and could live for centuries. Short-lived species tend to grow quickly and reach maturity faster than longer-lived species.

Bear in mind, however, that in urban environments, many trees and shrubs have their lives shortened by poor conditions, such as compacted soils beneath sidewalks.

'Hakura Nishiki' willow

How long will it take my tree to reach its full size?

Lois ❖ When you choose a tree or a shrub, years to maturity should be one of your considerations. Staff at your local nursery should be able to provide specific information about the variety you've chosen.

Jim ❖ Time to maturity depends on how big the tree was when it was transplanted, its species, and its local environment. A fast-growing tree like a tower poplar may reach its full height in as little as a decade. A bur oak, on the other hand, could take 60 years.

Here are some growth rates for the sake of comparison. Under ideal conditions, a bur oak, a slow-growing species, will gain 5–30 cm per year; a Norway spruce, a medium-growing species, will gain 25–50 cm; and a northwest poplar, a fast-growing species, will gain 50–100 cm or more.

Why do some trees and shrubs live longer than others?

Jim ❖ Some species are genetically predisposed to live longer than others, but environment also plays a big role. Environmental factors include soil, water, sunlight, and injury from insects, disease or improper pruning. Problems in the environment—injury by insects, for example, or prolonged drought—may reduce a tree or shrub's life expectancy.

When do flowers begin to form for the next growing season?

Jim ❖ Spring-flowering shrubs form flower buds late in the growing season and bloom as soon as the weather warms in the spring. However, their buds need to accumulate enough hours of chilling during the winter before they'll bloom.

Summer-flowering shrubs form buds on the new branches that emerge early in the season and bloom later, in the summer.

Why don't trees and shrubs bloom all summer?

Lois ❖ Trees and shrubs flower to enhance pollination by insects or animals, with the ultimate goal of producing seeds. A tree or shrub naturally blooms at the best time for that species to reproduce; the entire growing season may not suit its needs.

As well, less breeding work has been done to extend the blooming period of trees and shrubs (compared to, say, bedding plants). We just have to enjoy the flowers while they bloom!

Jim ❖ Trees and shrubs don't exist to satisfy the desires of people. They bloom in order to reproduce. Each tree and shrub has evolved its own strategy for successfully producing seeds.

If a plant blooms too early in the season, a frost might halt seed production before it even has a chance to start. At that time, pollinating insects like bees may not yet be flying. If the plant flowers too late in the season, it won't have enough time to set seed before the cold weather sets in.

How much sun do trees need?

Lois ❖ As much as they can get! Trees that receive inadequate sunlight produce fewer leaves. They may even die if light levels drop too low. Think about a forest and where you see trees growing in it. The largest, strongest, healthiest trees receive lots of sunlight.

Jim ❖ There are no hard and fast rules for trees and sunlight, but I suggest at least six hours of direct sunlight per day. Light is a plant's energy source. With plentiful light, a tree will thrive. If a tree receives only enough light to match the energy it expends, it won't put on any new growth. If it receives less light energy than it uses, the tree eventually dies.

CHAPTER 2 ❧
CHOOSING TREES AND SHRUBS

Choosing the right tree or shrub for your yard requires some thought. Of course you must pick the plants that appeal most to your aesthetic sense, but keep the plants' requirements in mind, too. Many years ago, we planted a row of poplars and several rows of apples behind the house, but we didn't realize the apples were too close to the poplars. As the poplars matured, they gradually shaded out the apple trees and eventually caused the death of all but the most distant row of apples. A hard lesson, but well worth learning!

Zones

What's a zone?

Lois ❖ Zones are regions that have similar climates. The lower the zone number, the lower the temperature drops in winter. Zone 10 is frost-free year-round, and zone 0 has permafrost and extremely cold winters. Canada is unusual because of its wide range of climatic zones: Victoria is zone 9, while Resolute Bay is zone 0.

Jim ❖ Zones are further divided into "a" and "b," with the "b" sub-zone being five degrees colder in winter than "a." Zone ratings are used as a guideline for determining whether a plant will survive in a particular region. As a rule, the higher the zone number, the greater the number of plants that will survive the winter, but this is not always the case.

How do I know what zone I live in?

Lois ❖ Simply find your community on a climate-zone map. Zone maps are regularly published in gardening magazines and product catalogues. Garden centres also have zone maps, and maps can be found on various websites.

Jim ❖ The map gives the official answer. However, in practice, you often find several different climatic conditions in a single region or, in the case of a single yard, a mini-microclimate! Trees themselves can be responsible for creating microclimates; old growth forests are a perfect example.

I live in zone 4 but want to try some more tender shrubs. Can I try shrubs rated to zones 5 and 6?

Lois ❖ I always reserve space in my yard for out-of-zone plant trials. Keep in mind that there are numerous "microclimates" within a zone. Microclimates exist in backyards and gardens because of the shelter provided by houses, the "heat island" effect of cities, and the shelter of trees themselves. I've found that growing plants from one zone higher is successful in many instances. I've had less success with plants from two zones higher, but many trials are still warranted. Success is rare when you push three zones higher, but it can be a lot of fun trying.

Jim ❖ Zone hardiness ratings serve as a guideline for determining which plants are likely to do well in a particular zone, but don't rely on them exclusively. Many plants defy their official zone ratings and thrive in somewhat harsher climates. Remember also that different catalogues may list zone ratings differently; the ratings are not absolute categories.

Zone ratings are based by and large on absolute winter lows, but other factors, like moisture and snow cover, greatly influence a tree or shrub's ability to survive. Trial and error is still the only sure method of finding out.

Some gardeners who live in really cold winter climates treat plants like hybrid tea roses as annuals. Harvesting a bouquet of flowers is reward in itself to offset having to plant the shrubs each year.

Will any trees survive in zone 1?

Jim ❖ Yes, but your choices are somewhat limited. Several species of spruce, poplar, and willow survive in zone 1, but the harsh climate results in slower growth and often a smaller mature size.

Shopping for Trees and Shrubs

What are the major factors I should consider when choosing trees and shrubs?

Lois ❖ Here's my quick list:

- Hardiness: will it survive and thrive where you live?
- Size and shape: is it suitable for your available space?
- Variety traits: colour, blooming time, and texture of foliage and bark.
- Undesirable traits: dropping fruit, suckering, invasive growth habit.
- Neighbours: will your choice of tree affect their property?
- Hazards: could it endanger your family, pets, or property in any way?

Most importantly, do you like the look of the tree or shrub? That above all should guide your decision.

Jim ❖ I'd add a few factors to Mom's list. You might want to consider the tree or shrub's growing requirements (water, sunlight, fertilizer), its intended purpose (to screen, to provide shade, or as a feature in the landscape), and the maintenance required to keep it looking good.

When I'm looking at a whole nursery full of trees, how do I decide which one to buy?

Lois ❖ First, decide what you are trying to achieve in your yard. For example, if you know you want a tree about three metres high and two metres wide at maturity to block out an ugly view, you can quickly narrow down your choices. Then you can look at other features you have in mind, such as fall colour.

People often fall in love with a tree in a nursery, plant it in the yard, and watch in horror as it outgrows its location. If you're planting an entire yard, by all means draw up a landscape plan. It will save you a lot of headaches in the future.

Jim ❖ It's really worthwhile to do a little research before you head down to the local nursery. The more information you have, the better choice you can make—and you won't make a decision that you'll regret later. There are all kinds of resources out there from books and magazines to websites. Talking to experienced fellow gardeners and certified nursery staff completes the picture.

Moving a basketed tree

Choosing the Right Tree

A majestic tree is often the focal point of a yard, with the potential to provide pleasure for many decades. I have particularly fond memories of a huge maple tree on the farm that served as a swing support and refuge from the summer sun. Of course, that tree was already a few decades old when Mom and Dad moved to the farm. Many of today's homeowners aren't lucky enough to have big, beautiful trees in the yard, and their only option is to purchase one.

When you buy a tree, there are several factors to take into consideration to ensure its health and longevity. Most importantly, always choose a tree that will fit your yard. As obvious as this advice seems, many people discover that a poorly chosen tree quickly overtakes their lot.

golden elder

Next, look at the tree form. Branches should be uniformly spaced around the trunk, not predominantly on one side or the other. Examine the branch angles. The branches should not be growing at acute angles to the trunk unless it's characteristic of that particular species (for instance, the tower poplar). Branches growing at acute angles are weakly attached to the trunk and may break off in a windstorm.

Never choose a tree with codominant stems, that is, a tree with a trunk that forks. Such trees split easily; always choose a tree with a single, strong central leader. Watch out for large cracks or cankers: they're entry points for insects and disease, and may indicate an existing infection.

'Red Splendor' crabapple

Now check the base of the tree, immediately below the soil, for girdling roots. Girdling roots are roots that outgrow the pot and, having nowhere else to go, encircle the tree stem. They must be removed before transplanting.

Check the root ball. The bigger the root mass, the better; trees with a small root ball relative to above-ground growth often suffer a great deal of transplant shock. Ensure the roots are moist.

Take the time to inspect the tree carefully before you buy. The care you invest now will ensure that you and your tree enjoy a long and happy association.

American mountain ash

Clanbrassiliana spruce 'Carol Mackie' daphne

When is the best time to shop for trees? When is it too late for it to be worthwhile?

Lois ❖ The first question has different meanings to different people. If you want the best selection, shop in the spring. If you're after the best possible price, wait until fall.

Trees planted in spring and summer establish their root systems more quickly, but I've had great success planting many species in the fall. As long as you can work the soil, it's not too late to plant.

Jim ❖ It's too late to shop when you can't dig! Many trees and shrubs can be planted, container and all, in a holding bed over the winter (an empty vegetable bed works well). Be sure to water them in very well. As soon as possible in the spring, dig them up, remove the pot, and plant them in their new permanent home. Late-fall planting or planting when a tree or shrub is dormant is fine. Watering is key because roots confined in a container can't reach the moisture in the soil around them.

Where should I shop? What features should I look for in a greenhouse or garden centre?

Lois ❖ Look for a nursery that offers knowledgeable service to help you make the right choices, a wide selection of trees and shrubs, a clean facility that ensures you're not taking home serious diseases or insect pests, and a guarantee to back the product.

Jim ❖ The health of the trees and shrubs that are for sale will indicate a lot about the place itself. If the plants look healthy and well cared for, and the staff can answer your questions, you're in the right place.

Should I buy small trees and shrubs or more mature ones?

Lois ❖ It depends on your patience and your budget. The larger the tree, the more expensive it will be—and prices go up rapidly for every centimetre of additional trunk diameter. You pay more for a large tree because the nursery has had to care for it for many more years than a small specimen.

Jim ❖ A large tree gives you the advantage of getting an almost-instant "finished" plant, but there are drawbacks. The larger the tree, the more roots (proportionately) that are removed when the tree is dug from the field. Many trees do not adapt well to having so many roots removed, and they either die or do not put on any growth for several years until the roots become established.

If you buy a very large tree, you also have to consider transportation costs. You can move a small tree in a car trunk or pickup, but to move a big one you'll have to hire a large truck and tree spade.

If you're looking for a tree of a certain height, you may want to consider a smaller, fast-growing variety that will achieve your goal sooner than a larger but slower-growing variety.

When I'm shopping, how can I tell which trees are healthy?

Jim ❖ This can be tricky. Here is a checklist of important features:
- Are the leaves or leaf buds healthy?
- Do the branch tips look healthy?
- Is the trunk free of large scars?
- Is the root ball moist and intact?
- Are there any girdling roots?

Keep in mind that after being shipped long distances, trees and shrubs can look a little sad, but they should perk up with thorough watering and exposure to sunlight. Buy from a reputable nursery that backs its plants with a solid guarantee.

Are there grades of trees and shrubs?

Jim ❖ Grades are designations or expectations of performance associated with a specific plant group; these standards may include size, quality, and historical details like age. Growers may establish their own grades. That is, a specimen that represents a grade A or #1 for one grower may be a grade B or #2 for another; the selling price will often reflect the quality.

In Canada, we refer to the Canadian Standards for Nursery Stock. These standards are assigned by the Canadian Nursery Trades Association and include expectations for size, root ball-to-height ratios, and branching.

Is it better to buy potted or burlapped trees?

Lois ❖ Both containers and burlap are fine. What matters more is the tree's general health and the care it has received at the nursery. Balled and burlapped trees dry out faster than potted trees, but if the nursery has watered them thoroughly and regularly, they will be fine.

Jim ❖ The ratio of shoot to root is critical. In other words, the above-ground portion of the plant (the shoot) must be balanced with the below-ground portion (the roots). Trees that have disproportionately small root systems may die or establish very poorly in your yard.

When a large tree is grown in a small pot, the risk of root girdling increases dramatically. This means that the roots can begin to grow around the main stem, literally choking the tree. When planting under these conditions, gently unwind and spread out the fine roots. Thick girdling roots must be removed to prevent severe damage to the tree.

With burlapped trees, a small root ball means that far too many roots have been removed relative to the above-ground growth. As a result, the tree is under a great deal of stress and is much more likely to die after transplanting. Look for a large, moist, well-wrapped root ball.

Why are some trees so expensive?

Lois ❖ Some trees grow very slowly and take years to reach marketable size. Many trees have been grown and nurtured in fields for more than a decade before being sold. Water, fertilizer, weed control, pest control, transplanting, potting, digging, and shipping are all expensive. That's why large trees are substantially—and justifiably—more expensive than saplings.

Jim ❖ It can also be a question of the kind of tree you're purchasing. If it is rare or unusual, or if only limited stock is available, the price will rise accordingly.

Should I insure my trees for replacement value? If so, how do I know what they're worth?

Lois ❖ Check with your insurance agent. A percentage of your home-owner's policy may cover damage to landscaping, but it can be difficult to determine the value of established trees. Replacement value of trees is based on a complicated formula involving species, size and age, location, availability, and transplanting costs. If you have a particular reason for concern, you might also want to check with a lawyer.

Trees, Shrubs, and Neighbours

One of the most common complaints we hear goes something like this: "My neighbour's tree is shedding needles all over my lawn..." The problem is that plants don't respect property lines.

For example, it is not at all uncommon for the roots or branches of a large tree to encroach on a neighbour's property. Usually, this is merely annoying. Overhanging branches may shed needles, fruit, or leaves onto the lawn, creating a bit more raking work in the fall. However, invading branches can also shade out vegetables and bedding plants, hampering their growth. Roots sneaking under fences into your yard can drain precious resources from plants, or even create cracks in sidewalks and foundations. According to *Arboriculture and the Law in Canada* by Julian Dunster and Susan Murray, if intruding roots damage a neighbour's house, the tree owner can be held liable.

What can you do? Dunster and Murray state that homeowners have the right to cut roots or branches that cross over the property line—but only at the property line, no further. Cutting beyond the property line (on the side of the tree owner) technically constitutes trespassing. Interestingly, any plant material that hangs into a neighbour's yard still belongs to the owner of the tree. As I understand it, if one were to follow the letter of the law, cut branches and fruit should be returned to the owner of the tree, not kept by the pruner. (In practice, I would hope that most neighbours are more reasonable.)

Of course, cutting back roots or branches to the property line may create a major problem: an unsightly, weakened tree that may die. While you have the right to cut back an intruding tree, consider that you may be liable if the tree dies: the law, thus far, is unclear on liability in cases like these.

Even if you escape having to pay for a replacement tree, you could face some hard feelings.

More importantly, a weakened tree could potentially become a hazardous tree. Hazardous trees present serious problems. According to what I've learned, if a tree falls and damages people or property, one of the following things could happen: if the tree looked healthy and the owner

was taking reasonable care of it before the incident, there is probably no liability. If the tree was obviously weakened and dangerous, the owner will likely be held liable. Finally, if a certified arborist or other qualified official warned the owner that the tree was dangerous, but the advice was ignored, the owner is almost certainly liable. It is worth your while, then, to work with your neighbour to repair or remove damaged trees before they collapse or become too intrusive.

The best way to avoid difficulty is to communicate with your neighbours. Difficulties can be smoothed over much more easily when the people over the fence are friends rather than strangers. Discuss other options before cutting off a neighbour's branches. Perhaps he'll let you keep the fruit, or offer to help rake when fall comes. Maybe you'll trade some cuttings or divided perennials. It's not a bad idea to discuss major new plantings, too—your neighbour might point out potential problems you hadn't considered, or she might suggest planting a common hedge.

trees and shrubs with distinctive foliage

'Purple Rain' birch
buffaloberry
'Golden Champion'
    cedar
'Schubert' chokecherry
'Thunderchild'
    crabapple
'Carol Mackie' daphne
golden variegated
    dogwood
yellow-leaf dogwood
most elders
    (except red-berried
    and 'Adams')
'Gold Prince' euonymus
'Golden Pin Cushion'
    false cypress
'Sungold' false cypress
blue fir
juniper (most varieties)
'Crimson King' maple
Swedish mayday
'Dart's Gold' ninebark
golden ninebark
'Blue Shag' pine
'French Blue Scotch'
    pine
Russian olive
silver poplar
salt bush
sea buckthorn
'Goldmound' spirea
'Magic Carpet' spirea
creeping blue spruce
'Fat Albert' spruce
'Hoopsi' spruce
'Montgomery' spruce
'Hakura Nishiki' willow
'Polar Bear' willow
silver willow

creeping blue spruce

Why do some of the plant tags give different height/bloom information than the signs in my garden centre?

Lois ❖ Plant tags rarely address all the regions. The staff at your local nursery will be able to give you a better idea of what to expect in your region.

Jim ❖ Final plant heights and blooming season can vary enormously depending on the region. Shade trees like the sugar maple may grow to 100 feet in moist, long-season regions of the eastern US and Canada, but only half that height in the drier, shorter season of the western plains.

Blooming seasons are also affected greatly by region. Canada's west coast, for example, may have its last spring frost in March while other regions may not have their last frost until early or late May. As a result, blooming on the coast could be a month or two earlier than it is inland.

Choosing Trees and Shrubs

What are some trees and shrubs with interesting foliage?

Lois ❖ Interesting could refer to leaf colour, shape, size, and texture, and I like to think of bark and blooms as well. A tree or shrub's interest can also be heightened by contrasting or complementing it with other plants. The list at left suggests some distinctive species.

I would like to plant an unusual or rare tree variety. Any suggestions?

Jim ❖ Sometimes what is rare in one area is common in another. Rarity is frequently based on hardiness. For example, people living in zone 8 or 9 may try to grow a banana tree that may be very common in tropical zone 10. A banana tree growing in zone 8 would be rare.

True rarity is a plant that is uncommon anywhere in the world, either because it's difficult to propagate or because it has highly specific growing requirements. Check with your local garden centre for recommendations of some locally rare trees and shrubs.

What trees and shrubs have good fall colour?

Lois ❖ The chart at right lists some of my favourites.

Jim ❖ The fall colour display depends on the species of tree and the weather conditions during late summer and early fall. Bright, sunny days and cool nights increase the production of pigments, triggering the most vibrant fall colours. Anthocyanins and carotenoids are present but masked in the leaves by the presence of chlorophyll (the predominant green in leaves). As fall approaches, the chlorophyll is absorbed by the tree, revealing the other colourful pigments.

I'd like a small shrub with bright-red fall colour. What do you recommend?

Lois ❖ You can't go wrong with the burning bush. As its name implies, it puts on a fantastic show of fiery red in the fall.

Jim ❖ Burning bush always looks great in the fall, but it will be at its fiery best if the early fall conditions include sunny, warm days followed by cool nights without hard frosts.

trees and shrubs for fall colour

ash
aspen
azalea
birch
burning bush
'Autumn Magic'
   chokecherry
cotoneaster
Siberian crabapple
cranberry
dogwood
elm
ginkgo
hazelnut
larch
linden
Manitoba maple
maple
mountain ash
nannyberry
Ohio buckeye
plum
double-flowing plum
poplar
serviceberry
snowball
sumac
wayfaring tree

'Rosy Lights' azalea

shade-tolerant trees & shrubs

Remember that "shade-tolerant" means exactly that: the plant can stand a degree of shade, but it still needs a certain amount of direct sun.

arrowwood
sun to partial shade
American bittersweet
sun to shade
bog rosemary
sun to part shade
boxwood ('Alberta,'
'Green Mountain,'
'Wintergreen')
sun to light shade
Ohio buckeye
sun to part shade
cedar ('Boisbriand,'
'Brandon,' 'Golden
Champion,' 'Golden
Globe,' 'Holmstrup,'
'Rushmore,' 'Wareana,'
'Woodwardi,' 'Yellow
Ribbon')
sun to part shade
cranberry ('Compactum'
and 'Dwarf European)
sun or shade
daphne ('Briggs
Moonlight')
part shade
dogwood *light shade*
euonymus
(several varieties)
sun or shade
hawthorn
sun to part shade
juniper ('Little Rocket,'
'Bar Harbor,' 'Dwarf
Japanese, 'Arcadia,'
'Variegata,'
'Cologreen')
sun to part shade
serviceberry
sun to part shade
spirea *sun to light shade*

Do any trees tolerate shade?

Jim ❖ Trees always grow better in full sun, but some can tolerate a degree of shade. Shade in this case means growing underneath a tree canopy. Balsam fir, white spruce, sugar maple, 'Pagoda' dogwood, Tatarian maple, and amur maple will tolerate some shade while they are young; see the list at left for more suggestions.

Can I grow any trees or shrubs in full shade?

Lois ❖ Everyone I talk with seems to have one spot in their yard where nothing wants to grow. If possible, increase the light levels in this area by pruning any surrounding trees. If the shade is so dense that even weeds won't grow in this spot, your money is probably better spent on bark mulch or decorative rock, or you could add a non-plant feature such as a birdbath or statuary.

Jim ❖ Full shade implies an area that receives no sunlight. No trees or shrubs will grow in these conditions. As the sunlight increases, so do your options.

Every plant needs a certain amount of light energy in order to grow. This is determined both by the intensity and the duration of the sunlight that reaches the leaves. Although plants can adapt somewhat to lower light levels by developing larger (but thinner) leaves to intercept more sunlight, more often than not they will become leggy or stretched and have sparse foliage.

'Tor' spirea

What evergreen plants tolerate hot, dry weather and poor soil conditions?

Jim ❖ Limber and ponderosa pines are some of the toughest. Many species of juniper can also survive in hot, dry, sandy soils with little organic matter. But even though they tolerate these conditions, they will grow better and look healthier with more moisture and richer soil. Rather than choose a tree for these conditions, you might be better off to amend the soil.

salt bush

What is a good shrub for dry soils?

Lois ❖ Buffaloberry is an excellent drought-tolerant shrub. See the list at right for some other attractive choices.

I want to grow trees at our cabin at the lake, but I can't always be there to water them. Are any varieties particularly drought resistant?

Lois ❖ Many varieties can get by with little or no extra care, once they become well established. However, if you're transplanting trees—even those that are drought resistant—they need regular watering until they become established, which usually takes about a year.

After the first year, any additional watering will increase the growth and vigour. Remember, just because a plant tolerates drought doesn't mean that it prefers it!

Jim ❖ Start with small potted trees, because their roots are largely intact and therefore better able to adapt to a drier environment. But Mom's right: they will still need regular watering until they are well established, and will benefit from regular watering throughout their lives. You might also want to try tree-watering rings (a drip-irrigation system).

trees and shrubs for hot, dry locations

amur maackia
ash
buffaloberry
caragana
cherry prinsepia
currant
genista
hackberry
honeysuckle
juniper
pincherry
pine
potentilla
Russian olive
salt bush
sea buckthorn
spruce
sumac

trees and shrubs for erosion control

caragana
cotoneaster
currant
cutleaf stephanandra
euonymus
genista
juniper (all spreading
    varieties)
lilac (all suckering
    varieties)
dwarf Chinese
    mountain ash
'Tilden Parks' ninebark
Russian cypress
'Gro-low' sumac
willow

trees and shrubs for wet areas

alder
ash
birch
bog rosemary
'Autumn Magic'
    chokecherry
dogwood
elm
holly
larch
red maple
silver maple
pin oak
poplar
willow

What shrubs would you suggest for erosion control and ground cover?

Lois ❖ Shrubs that root where their branches touch the soil or that sucker and spread profusely work well to control erosion. See the list at left for suggestions.

Jim ❖ Any plant will reduce erosion to a certain extent, simply because its roots hold the soil. Erosion problems occur primarily on slopes and in ravines and gullies.

What can I grow in wet areas?

Jim ❖ Some trees will thrive in sites where water pools periodically, in heavy clay soils with poor drainage, and in sites that rarely dry out completely. See the list below, at left.

What trees or shrubs can I plant in acidic soil?

Jim ❖ There are several trees and shrubs that grow well in soils with a pH of less than 6.0. See the chart on page 39.

Which trees are most frost tolerant?

Jim ❖ Frost tolerance is a complex subject when it involves trees. It starts with cold tolerance. A tree like an aspen poplar might survive -60°C in the dead of winter, while a peach tree will only tolerate lows of about −20°C (depending on the variety). This cold tolerance is related to the genetic makeup of the tree.

What isn't often understood is that a tree's cold tolerance changes depending on the time of year. The peach tree that is hardy to -20°C in the dead of winter gradually "de-hardens" as spring approaches. So, theoretically, in early January it is at its maximum hardiness of -20°C. By February, this may be only -15°C, by March, -10°C, and so on. Once the tree buds begin to swell, they may be hardy only to -1°C. At this point, a hard frost might destroy the flower buds, meaning that the tree won't bear fruit that year (although, fortunately, it will regenerate its leaves). Thus, overall frost tolerance is relative to the time of year.

Where I live, the winters are bitterly cold. What kind of shade tree can I grow without fear of winter dieback?

Jim ❖ Green ash trees grow quite rapidly and can take the cold. Unfortunately, they leaf out late in the spring and drop their leaves early, so they don't provide shade for much of the season compared to other shade trees.

I'd like a fast-growing columnar tree for my backyard. Any recommendations?

Lois ❖ Swedish columnar aspen and tower poplar are excellent, trouble-free, fast-growing trees that look great and require no pruning.

Jim ❖ We've had tower poplars growing near the farmhouse for over twenty years. They've grown to over 10 m tall and have required absolutely no care beyond the work of the initial transplanting.

Which trees and shrubs are poisonous?

Jim ❖ Every tree is poisonous, if you eat enough of it. It's the dose that makes the poison, regardless of whether the substance is strychnine, wine, or sumac.

People often ask this question because they're afraid that their children or pets might ingest poisonous tree parts. Fortunately, most poisonous plants are bitter and unpalatable. Choking is still the number-one hazard, not toxicity.

trees & shrubs for acidic areas

alder
arrowwood
azaela
birch
bog rosemary
cedar
daphne
eastern white pine
fir
hemlock
holly
juniper
larch
rhododendron
Russian cypress
serviceberry
spruce

paper birch

Why do nurseries sell trees and shrubs that are invasive or suckering?

Lois ❖ One gardener's idea of an undesirable trait is another's answer to a gardening dilemma! For example, suckering may be an undesirable trait on a small city lot but exactly what's needed for erosion control on a country lot's hillside.

Jim ❖ You'd be hard pressed to find a tree (or a person, for that matter) without at least one characteristic that might be considered undesirable. Some trees produce fruit that stains driveways, others flower too early or too late, still others grow too large. Suckering is simply one more trait to take into consideration.

'Miss Canada' lilac

Enjoying Lilacs

Two of my favourite lilacs were developed in Canada by Dr. William Cumming, who once worked for the Morden Research Centre in Manitoba. **'Minuet'** is a fine lilac, with light-pink single flowers and lush green foliage. It's a non-suckering variety, too, and grows 3-4 m tall. **'Miss Canada'** is a 3 m tall and wide bush with stunning single blooms of magnificent magenta. Both varieties combine beauty with hardiness and are excellent choices for the yard.

Other great varieties include the famous **'President Lincoln,'** with its deep-blue double flowers; **'Pocahontas,'** an early-blooming, Manitoba-developed variety with maroon flowerbuds that open to deep-violet flowers; and **'Dwarf Korean,'** which starts showing off its profuse clusters of pinkish white blooms at age three, years earlier than most other lilacs.

'Dwarf Korean' lilac

And there are new lilac varieties to look for. **'Prairie Petite'** is a dwarf lilac, perfect for small shrub beds or borders. This variety has showy light-pink flowers and is heat and drought tolerant. **'Wedgewood Blue,'** another showy lilac, bears large clusters of lilac-pink buds that open to true-blue flowers with terrific fragrance. **'Wonder Blue'** is a compact shrub with very showy masses of sky-blue flowers.

'President Lincoln' lilac (left), 'Chinese' lilac (top)

Identifying specific varieties

Which tree has soft, ridged bark?

Lois ❖ You're probably thinking of the cork tree. The bark has deeply ridged, lightly coloured bark with a wonderfully soft texture.

Jim ❖ But don't stick any notes to it! This cork tree isn't the same tree that cork is harvested from. The cork found in wine bottles and bulletin boards is actually harvested from a species of oak tree.

What is that early spring-flowering, low-growing shrub with the powerful fragrance?

Lois ❖ It sounds like you're talking about the daphne. No shrub can match its powerful fragrance.

Jim ❖ The daphne also has lots of beautiful pink flowers, which look stunning in the early spring.

Which shrub in my yard smells like cinnamon?

Lois ❖ It's probably a flowering currant.

Is there an early-flowering shrub with yellow flowers?

Lois ❖ With its beautiful and abundant bright-yellow flowers, forsythia provides an excellent display of early spring colour. The flowering branches look great in cutflower bouquets, too.

I have an evergreen that spreads like a juniper but has soft foliage that resembles a cedar's. What is it?

Lois ❖ That sounds like a Russian cypress.

CHAPTER 3 🌾
GROWING TREES AND SHRUBS

*There's a saying that goes, "To plant a $50
tree, dig a $100 hole." That's a good way
to approach tree and shrub planting. Invest
at least as much effort in preparing your
planting site as you do in choosing your tree
or shrub. Choose your location wisely,
prepare a big hole with sloping rather than
vertical sides, and plant the base of the
trunk at soil level. Keep these basic steps in
mind and you can plant with confidence.*

My yard is bare and my budget is limited. How can I fill my yard with trees?

Lois ❖ The easiest way to add trees and shrubs to your yard is to buy them from a good nursery or garden centre and plant them carefully. Most nurseries offer a wide selection of varieties, sizes, and prices, and you can shop strategically if your budget requires it.

Jim ❖ Trees and shrubs can be grown and propagated in many ways. Each method is used to achieve a specific outcome, as each has specific advantages and disadvantages. See the chart on page 45.

How do growers produce so many plants so quickly?

Lois ❖ Growers continuously root cuttings and use tissue culture year after year for a steady supply of healthy trees and shrubs. Although the process may appear quick to the observer, it actually requires years of patience and investment.

Jim ❖ Nurseries plan years in advance to have a specific amount stock of trees and shrubs, and they use a variety of methods to ensure that supply. Growing from seed is one approach, but by far the most popular methods are cuttings and tissue culture. Once the supply has been created, the grower or the nursery raises the stock until it reaches saleable size.

When is the best time to propagate my trees and shrubs?

Jim ❖ It depends on the species. Spring is the usual time, but that doesn't apply to every species. Your choice will also be determined to some degree by the propagation method you choose; see the chart on page 45.

'Galahad' mock orange

Method	Advantage	Disadvantage
Growing from seed	• inexpensive • rewarding to start right from seed	• hard to find • needs special treatments • takes a long time • seeds from many plants produced from cuttings will not reproduce "true-to-type"
Planting seedlings and saplings	• ready to go—just plant and provide regular care	• more expensive than seed • although faster than seed to reach maturity, still quite slow
Moving an established tree	• shorter wait for tree to reach mature size	• can be exceedingly expensive • requires specialized equipment • can be a significant shock to tree
Dividing	• very inexpensive	• most trees and shrubs cannot be divided • takes several years to recover • greater risk of disease at division point
Propagating from stem cuttings	• inexpensive • easy to handle or move	• takes a long time for plants to reach large size • many cuttings are difficult to root • needs supplies (soil, trays, etc) • limited source material • many plants are grafted
Propagating from root cuttings	• inexpensive • doesn't affect appearance of above-ground growth	• not all plants can be root propagated • requires a bit more work to dig up suitable roots
Air layering	• will produce a large plant quickly	• mostly for indoor tropical plants, not suitable for outdoor plants • may destroy the original plant in many cases
Grafting	• can get multiple plants on one plant • can take advantage of mother plant's characteristics (hardiness, dwarfing, disease resistance)	• can have a plant that is totally non-uniform • grafting can only take place between compatible plants • takes a fair bit of skill
Tissue culture	• lots of plants from a small piece of tissue • identical to one another • can be pest free	• requires a lab and expensive materials • requires skill and knowledge

Starting Trees and Shrubs from Seed

How difficult is it to grow trees from seed?

Lois ❖ It varies tremendously from species to species, and it can be quite challenging. Some of the easier species to grow from seed are caragana, green ash, Manitoba maple, mountain ash, spruce, and pine.

Jim ❖ The challenge you face when you try to grow trees from seed is duplicating the environment in which the seed naturally germinates and grows. Those conditions include timing, temperature, moisture levels, and soil. Some trees produce sterile seeds because of hybridization, while others are male clones and don't produce seeds. Some hybrid seed is genetically unstable and may not produce the same type of tree.

So if you enjoy a challenge, do some research, choose a species, and give it a try; however, don't count on the results your first time out. I recommend fast-growing flowering shrubs such as roses, azaleas, and weigela for your initial experiments.

Why are some seeds sterile?

Jim ❖ When two plants hybridize, they occasionally produce seeds with an odd number of chromosomes (i.e., triploid). Triploid plants are often sterile.

How long does it take to grow a tree from seed?

Lois ❖ Trees grow at different rates depending on the species and the environment. Young trees often start growing quickly but slow down as they reach maturity.

Jim ❖ In an ideal environment, fast-growing trees might gain 60–150 cm in a year. Moderate growth falls in the 30–60 cm range. A slow-growing tree gains less than 30 cm per year. In other words, the growth rate depends on the tree you're trying to grow.

What do I need to do to grow my own trees from seed?

Lois ❖ You will need all of the same supplies that you would need to start bedding plants: seedling trays, grow lights or a bright, sunny window, seedling mix, vermiculite, fertilizer, pest-control products, and a good misting bottle.

Jim ❖ You'll also need a refrigerator or outdoor location to stratify seed. Just bear in mind that even with all the right equipment, germination may not be successful. Treat growing from seed as an experiment and you can learn a great deal.

Stratifying Seeds

Many species that we grow from seed thrive in a consistently warm and moist environment, so naturally, this is the kind of environment gardeners try to give their seeds. Seeds that refuse to germinate under these supposedly ideal conditions can be really frustrating. But this reluctance isn't stubbornness; rather, some seeds have evolved this trait to have the best chance of growing into a mature plant. The need for a long period of cold before sprouting is called stratification.

Take apple seeds, for example. It's futile to collect apple seeds in the fall with the intention of getting them to germinate immediately. That's because apple seed requires a long period of chilling temperatures in cold, moist soil. The seed will not germinate until it has lain dormant in such conditions for anywhere from several weeks to a few months. Chemicals in the seed that inhibit germination are gradually broken down by the cold; by the time the inhibiting chemicals are gone, spring has arrived, just in time for germination.

The reason for this mandatory chilling period, of course, is to give the seedling a fighting chance of survival. If the built-in dormancy period didn't exist, apple seeds would germinate all over the place in the fall, but the seedlings would be destroyed by the winter cold. Delphinium, larkspur, bells of Ireland, and Queen Anne's lace are other species that have this protective adaptation. Getting these seeds to germinate is relatively simple; just buy them early and chill them in the refrigerator at 0-10°C for several months before you plant.

male (at left) and female (at right) cones

Will trees re-seed themselves?

Lois ❖ Most trees will re-seed themselves. Otherwise, Mother Nature wouldn't be so successful!

Jim ❖ Not all trees will re-seed, for a variety of reasons. Some trees are male plants that don't produce seed, while some female plants produce seed but don't have a suitable male pollinator nearby (such as aspen poplar). Some species reproduce mainly by suckering, some hybrids produce sterile seed, and some trees grow in regions whose season is too short to produce viable seed.

Can I collect pine cones and plant the seeds?

Lois ❖ It is a long, slow process, but if you have the patience it can be fun and rewarding.

Jim ❖ In general, to get pine seeds to grow, you must extract the seeds sfrom the cones, stratify the collected seeds at 0–4°C for 1–3 months in moist perlite, then transplant the seedlings. Some pine species germinate very easily—almost as soon as you plant the seeds; other species must be stratified in cold conditions.

Planting Trees and Shrubs

What is a seedling tree?

Lois ❖ A seedling tree is a very small tree grown from seed. Nurseries often sell them to people who are buying in bulk and don't mind waiting for them to reach a larger size.

All of the trees used for evergreen reforestation are seedling trees, and most children receive seedling trees at school in Grade One. In the last few years, seedling trees have become popular gifts for guests at weddings.

What is a bare-root tree?

Lois ❖ A bare-root tree or shrub is grown in the field, stripped of soil, and then shipped to the customer. Provided that the plant is dormant (that is, it has not yet leafed out), it will transplant just as well as a tree with roots in soil and is often much cheaper.

Jim ❖ That said, you have much less flexibility with bare-root stock. You must plant it immediately upon receipt and early in the season; you cannot let it sit and dry out. Many nurseries have stopped selling bare-root stock because they can not guarantee that customers will plant quickly enough for the plant to survive.

Plants imported from outside of Canada and the US must be shipped bare-root because of concerns with pests in the soil. Provided it is packaged correctly to prevent moisture loss and is handled efficiently, bare-root stock transplants fairly successfully.

A bare-root tree

Should I remove the fibre or peat pot before I plant my tree?

Lois ❖ No. Remove the bottom of the fibre container, slash its side, and cut off the brim. The fibre is designed to rot in the soil fairly quickly. Leaving the brim of the pot above the soil will allow moisture to wick away from the roots. (Obviously, if the pot is plastic, it must be removed prior to planting.)

Jim ❖ It depends on the time of year you are planting. Growers pot plants in late winter. When the plants reach your local nursery, they will not have had sufficient time to develop many new roots and form a root ball that will stick together when the pot is removed. That's why they use a degradable pot. Later in the season, if the plant has developed a good root system, removing the pot won't be a problem. However, the container adds organic matter to the soil and certainly won't harm your tree if it's left on.

When can I begin planting trees?

Lois ❖ The sooner the better! Begin in the spring, as soon as you can work the soil.

When is a good time to plant container-grown trees and shrubs?

Lois ❖ You can plant container-grown plants any time from early spring right up until just a few weeks before freeze-up. Since container-grown plants have spent their entire lives in pots, all of their roots are intact.

Jim ❖ Take extra care when planting during the heat of summer. The tree or shrub will need to draw a lot of water from the soil, but it will not have rooted into its new location yet. Be sure to soak both the soil around the base and the surrounding soil thoroughly to encourage the development of new roots.

When is the latest I can plant trees in the fall?

Lois ❖ As a rule, I like to plant containerized plants up until a few weeks before freeze-up. From a practical perspective, it's nearly impossible to plant in frozen soil.

Jim ❖ In mild regions, it's essentially never too late to plant. The biggest danger in wet regions is poor site preparation. This can cause water to accumulate around the roots, starving them of oxygen.

When can I transplant a small evergreen?

Lois ❖ I've transplanted evergreens at all times of the year without a problem. This conflicts with conventional wisdom, but my practices sometimes do! It's important to water the newly transplanted tree daily for the first week.

Jim ❖ Professional growers don't transplant actively growing evergreens because the success rate declines in proportion to the size of the plant. Transplanting is done in the late winter to early spring, stopping as the plants begin to bud out and resuming again as the plants begin to go dormant.

After I bring my trees home, how long can I wait before planting them?

Lois ❖ It depends on how you've purchased your trees. If you have bare-root stock, plant them immediately. If the trees are balled and burlapped, you have a few weeks, provided you keep the root ball moist. If they're in containers, you can wait quite a while, as long as you water regularly.

Jim ❖ Mom's right; provided you keep the roots moist, you can hold off planting for weeks.

How do I plant my tree? What size hole should I dig?

Jim ❖ Don't think of it as simply digging a hole: think of it as preparing a planting site. When you plant a tree, you want it to root into the surrounding soil as quickly as possible. Prepare a soil area 4–5 times the diameter of the tree's root ball. For example, if your tree has a 30-cm root ball, prepare a site 120–150 cm wide. A well-prepared site of this size will allow the tree to establish its roots much more quickly and easily.

To prepare the soil, work in organic matter. Don't add so much that the soil becomes "peaty"; add just enough to loosen up any clay. Plant the tree so that the root ball is just below ground level; do not plant it deeper than its original soil level. Fill the hole with a mixture of garden soil and peat moss; firm lightly to remove air pockets. Leave a slight depression around the base of the tree. You can top with a shallow layer of mulch, but do not cover the base of the tree.

How to Plant Trees & Shrubs

1. Dig a hole the same height as and three times the width of the rootball.
2. Prepare a mixture of 80% garden soil and 20% peat moss.
3. Place enough mixture in the bottom of the hole to bring the rootball to just below ground level; firm to remove air pockets. Never plant a tree deeper than it is in the pot!

4. Mix fertilizer solution (Lois' Quick Start 10-52-10); 5 litres (one gallon) for every 30 centimeters of height or spread.
5. Gently loosen root ball and place plant in hole.
6. Fill hole with remaining soil mixture and firm to remove air pockets.

7. Leave a slight depression around plant and add fertilizer solution.
8. Add a shallow layer of mulch (bark or pine cones) to help retain soil moisture.
9. Water all trees and shrubs at least twice a week for the first growing season.

10. Water the area around the tree, not just the root ball.
11. If the water is thoroughly absorbed in less than 30 minutes, repeat the watering.
12. If the soil remains very wet between waterings, reduce the water volume by half, but maintain the same weekly schedule.

13. Fertilize with Lois' Quick Start 10-52-10 once a month until the end of July.

mountain alder

How deep do I plant balled and burlapped trees?

Jim ❖ Plant just to the original soil level. If you plant deeper, you risk suffocating the roots. The same rule applies to trees in containers: plant no deeper than the original soil level of the container.

Should I soak my tree before transplanting it?

Lois ❖ If the root ball is moist, there is no need to soak the roots.

Jim ❖ Water adds considerable weight to the root ball and makes transplanting more difficult. However, you must water the tree thoroughly immediately after planting. Don't forget to water the soil around the hole! Dry soil can pull water away from the root ball and delay rooting into the new soil.

Should I fertilize my trees after transplanting?

Lois ❖ The most crucial elements of successful transplanting are proper soil preparation and water. A starter fertilizer helps to promote root development, but it is not strictly required. I like to give my trees and shrubs the best start, so I fertilize at the time of planting.

Jim ❖ Gardeners tend to focus too much on fertilizer as the saviour of a transplanted tree but, as Mom says, the critical factors are proper site preparation and water. A light dose of fertilizer at transplanting will ensure an adequate supply of nutrients for tree growth.

What is transplant shock?

Lois ❖ Transplant shock is just a fancy term for stress. Many plants naturally suffer when they are moved, but with proper care they come through just fine. Symptoms of transplant shock include wilting of foliage and stems, slow growth, and even foliage drop. For instance, weeping larch will often drop all its needles after transplanting, but in a few weeks it should begin to regenerate new needles and recover fully.

Jim ❖ When you move a tree from one location to another, you end up removing as much as 95 percent of its root system. It's difficult to avoid this, because tree roots spread out a long distance from the trunk. Since roots are essential for absorbing moisture and nutrients, a newly transplanted tree is severely stressed until it can regenerate those lost roots. Water is the key to survival for these trees. Keep the soil around the tree consistently moist (but not saturated) until it gets re-established.

I kept my shrubs in my garage and they've started to turn yellow. Have I done something wrong?

Lois ❖ We call this "garage plant syndrome"! If you can't plant your trees or shrubs immediately after you bring them home, set them out during the day and only put them back in the garage at night if outside temperatures are expected to drop below freezing.

Jim ❖ Never leave a tree or shrub in the garage during the day when the temperature is above freezing. It won't take long for the leaves to turn yellow and drop off. In fact, the warmer the garage temperature, the quicker the leaves will turn yellow.

Outside, even on a cloudy day, your plants receive at least twice as much light as they do indoors in front of a bright, south-facing window. And the conditions outside help to prepare plants for transplanting. Keeping your plants out of the garage is just as important as keeping your car out of the garden!

How do I determine how far apart to set my trees?

Lois ❖ It depends on the species of the tree or shrub and its intended use. If you're making a hedge, keep the plants close together. If you're planting a specimen tree, be sure to leave room for a mature canopy.

Jim ❖ There is nothing worse than trees and shrubs crowded together unintentionally: they lose their symmetry and landscape value. Closely planted hedges and windbreaks look fine, though, because they are purposely planted close together.

How much space should I leave between a tree and a building?

Lois ❖ There are two important issues to consider:

- Aesthetics: a tree crowded up against a building will lose its natural symmetry. Branches close to the building may be stunted, may produce fewer leaves, or may even die.

- Potential damage: if the tree is too close to a building, the building may be at risk. Branches may damage windows, sap may stain siding, or the tree may eventually fall over.

To calculate the minimum space, take the true canopy spread of a mature tree and divide by two. For example, if a tree has a 10-m spread at maturity, plant it no closer than 5 m to a building.

Jim ❖ If you don't have a lot of space and you must plant closer to a building than you would like, choose a columnar or compact variety of tree. You can achieve pleasing results with these forms.

Contrary to popular belief, no tree can penetrate a sound foundation or sound sewer lines, but expanding roots can cause sidewalks to heave. Root barriers and proper site preparation can reduce this problem.

Moving Established Trees

How big should the root ball for my two-metre spruce tree be when I move it?

Jim ❖ The Canadian Nursery Trades Association recommends standards for the size of the root ball in relation to height and spread of the tree. A tall, broad conifer like a blue spruce that is two metres tall should have a root ball eighty centimetres in diameter.

Can I move a 25-foot cedar?

Jim ❖ Not easily! You would need a root ball 200 cm in diameter and 80 cm deep. The soil alone would weigh 2000 kg! The job would require a huge tree spade (a special truck-mounted shovel), and the cedar would likely die from transplant shock.

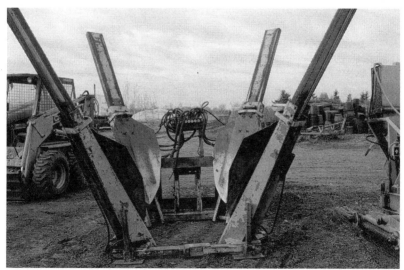

Moving a large tree requires the use of a tree spade.

I'm moving. Can I take my trees or shrubs with me?

Lois ❖ Many customers call us desperate to move a favourite tree or shrub because of an impending property sale. You must either move the plants before you list the property for sale or try to reach an agreement with the purchaser.

If you must move a tree or shrub when it's actively growing, there are a few steps you can take to improve the chances of transplanting it successfully:

• Preserve as much of the root ball as possible and ensure that the roots don't dry out.

• Have the plant's new location prepared before you dig it up, and transplant it as soon as possible.

• Be absolutely vigilant about maintaining an adequate level of moisture.

Jim ❖ First, you must consider the legal issues. Unless you made it clear that the trees and shrubs were not part of the sale agreement (which they normally are), it could be illegal to take them with you.

In terms of protecting your plants' health, you must consider several factors:

• Species: some species will make the move more successfully than others.

• Size: smaller trees are easier to move; large ones often can't be moved at all.

• Season: it's hard to relocate plants successfully during the heat of summer or in the dead of winter.

Division

Can I divide my shrubs?

Lois ❖ I don't recommend that you dig up and divide shrubs. There are better ways of propagating shrubs; division is rarely successful.

Jim ❖ When you divide a woody shrub, you risk irreparable damage to the roots. You also make the plant more prone to diseases and insects.

If your shrub has overgrown its location, a pruning program planned over several months or a couple of seasons can bring it under control. If you want to share the shrub with someone else, take a cutting; you're much more likely to succeed this way.

Growing Trees and Shrubs from Cuttings

Can I start my own shrubs from cuttings?

Lois ❖ You certainly can. Purchase a good book on propagation to help you with the specifics for each species, and be patient. Growing from cuttings can be a fascinating hobby, but it requires patience and perseverance.

Jim ❖ Taking cuttings from shrubs is not difficult, but timing and other factors play an important part in how successfully they take. A good reference book will give you the right information and is well worth the price if you're serious about propagating.

Can I take cuttings from my trees?

Lois ❖ Yes, but that's the easy part. Getting them to root is the trick! Some species, such as poplar and willow, root easily from cuttings. Others present a much greater challenge. My advice is to take lots of cuttings from various parts of the tree and try them at different times during the growing season.

Jim ❖ Mom's right, but a good book on plant propagation will save you years of learning by trial and error.

'Sweetberry' honeysuckle

How do I start a cutting?

Lois ❖ Take a cutting from new green shoots that have already leafed out in spring or early summer. The cutting should be about 15 cm long. Cut the low end of the branch on an angle to avoid planting the cutting upside down (polarity is important).

Remove the bottom leaves but be sure to leave at least three leaf nodes. Dip the cutting in a #1 or #2 rooting hormone, then place it in a porous rooting medium such as perlite. Mist the cutting and the medium regularly. The cutting should root within a few weeks; rooting time depends on a number of factors, including temperature and species. Once the roots appear, you can transplant the new plant as you would any seedling.

Jim ❖ If you take a very long cutting, you can divide it into several smaller cuttings provided you remember which end is up and plant accordingly. Professionals who use this method often dip the top of the cutting in wax to mark it and to prevent moisture loss.

Here are a few tips:

• Cuttings are best taken in midsummer from plants grown in full sun (they have higher energy reserves).

• Remove any flower buds from the cuttings.

• Dip the cuttings in rooting hormone.

• Root cuttings in soilless medium at 24°C, mounding the base to stimulate rooting.

I tried to take cuttings from my rhododendron but they didn't work. What went wrong?

Jim ❖ The general method described above works for most trees and shrubs (for instance, willow, lilac, and hydrangea). However, some species need special treatment. For example, rhododendron transpires excessively and needs to be defoliated before rooting. Consult a good book on plant propagation for species-specific advice. But don't be afraid to experiment with a few cuttings each season; you won't harm your plants, and you're certain to learn more about them.

Can I stick a willow branch in the ground and start a new tree?

Lois ❖ Yes. In greenhouses, willows root readily from cuttings. There is a much higher percentage of failure outdoors, however, so you'll need to use more cuttings.

Jim ❖ Willows naturally contain the right combination of compounds to help them root successfully. Cuttings planted in early spring root rapidly; summer cuttings also root well. As Mom says, greenhouses provide a superior rooting environment. If you do try to root willow outside, take lots of cuttings, insert them into loose soil, and then select those that develop vigorous roots.

What is rooting compound?

Jim ❖ Rooting compound contains growth regulators that increase the percentage of cuttings that form roots, hasten root initiation, increase the number and quality of roots produced per cutting, and increase overall uniformity of rooting. Plants whose cuttings root with difficulty benefit from the use of rooting compound.

How do I take root cuttings from my trees?

Jim ❖ Take root cuttings from trees and shrubs in late winter or early spring when the plants' energy reserves are highest. Cut a section of the root 5–8 cm long and plant it vertically in a soil–filled container. Keep the soil evenly moist but not wet. A new shoot should appear within a few weeks.

Can I use suckers from lilacs and other shrubs to grow new plants?

Lois ❖ If your tree or shrub produces suckers, you can often cut them out and move them to produce new plants. See the root-cutting method described above.

Jim ❖ Don't try this on a grafted plant! A grafted plant is actually made up of two distinct plants: the rootstock and the graft. If you take a sucker from below the graft, you'll be growing the rootstock, which is not the plant you actually want to propagate.

Layering

What is simple layering?

Lois ❖ Layering is a method of starting new plants without taking a cutting. A branch is bent so that a section can be buried in the soil. Bending, cutting, or girdling the "U" stimulates rooting at that spot. The buried section will form roots and can later be separated from the main plant.

What is air layering?

Jim ❖ Air layering entails stripping a section of bark from a desirable branch and covering the exposed section with moist material such as moss. Wrap the moss with material to keep the moisture in and secure it. The branch will send out roots into the moss; when they are well established, the new section can be severed from the main tree and planted.

This method is used almost exclusively on tropical plants in greenhouses or indoor environments.

Grafting

What is grafting?

Lois ❖ Grafting is the process of attaching a branch, bud, or root from one plant to another. The grafted material "knits" onto the grafted plants but maintains its own characteristics such as bloom colour and fruit. Grafting has a long and important history for plant enthusiasts, and today many trees and shrubs are sold grafted onto rootstock.

Jim ❖ The rootstock (the portion of the graft below the soil) develops into the root system of the grafted plant. The portion above the ground is called the scion.

Rootstocks are used for several reasons:

- They may have dwarfing characteristics, keeping the scion smaller and more manageable (for example, dwarf apples).
- They may be resistant to soil pests and disease.
- They may be particularly hardy.
- They may adapt well to growing in difficult soils.

Can I graft my own trees?

Lois ❖ Yes, you can. Grafting requires skill and proper tools, but many gardeners enjoy great success using this technique.

Jim ❖ The first step is to ensure compatibility between the rootstock and the scion. It's easiest to graft within a species, harder between genera, and harder still between families. Beginners should start with easy species like apples, and try many different grafts to ensure that some will take.

What are the different methods of grafting?

Lois ❖ There are several different grafting techniques, but the simplest is T-budding. A T-shaped cut is made in the rootstock. The new plant material is inserted into the cut, and the plants knit together.

Jim ❖ Another technique is to prepare the scion (the above-ground portion of the plant) by cutting the bottom end to a point or inverted V. Cut the top of the rootstock into a V and match the scion tip to it. Seal the joint to prevent moisture loss, using a biodegradable material such as wax, and secure the graft with tape. The time it takes for a graft to form depends on the species of plants being grafted and environmental conditions such as temperature. For the graft to be successful, the rootstock and scion must be compatible.

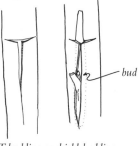

T-budding or shield-budding

wedge graft

Tissue Culture

What is tissue culture?

Lois ❖ Tissue culture is a propagation method that can create thousands of plants from clusters of cells. It is normally only employed by commercial growers. We have had a few difficult-to-propagate shrubs like spirea and Tigris roses propagated by tissue culture for sale at our greenhouse.

Jim ❖ The term tissue culture is being replaced by the term "micro-propagation." Micropropagation is done in a lab to mass-produce plants that may not otherwise be easily propagated. A tissue sample is taken and placed in a mixture of nutrients. These mixtures are highly specialized and often jealously guarded secrets. If the mixture is right, many little plantlets will grow from the callus tissue.

The trick with tissue culture is to get a cell or group of cells to initiate roots or shoots. If this can be accomplished with the special concotion of nutrients and hormones, the "micro" plants will grow into small seedlings that can be transplanted into pots.

Can I have my trees tissue cultured?

Lois ❖ No, for the most part it is not really feasible for home propagation. It requires a specialized lab and extensive knowledge.

Jim ❖ Some companies are offering tissue culture kits for adventurous home gardeners to experiment with some simpler-to-grow tissue culture plants.

Why do growers use tissue culture? Isn't seeding just as fast?

Jim ❖ The advantage of tissue culture is that you bypass all the difficulties of propagating from seed like stratification and scarifaction. You also produce many plants from a single piece of plant tissue without having to collect and store seed.

Another advantage for growers is the resulting plants are all identical copies or clones of one another. With seed, there can be a great deal of variability in the resulting plants.

silver willow

CHAPTER 4 ❧
THE GROWING SEASON

*The growing season offers many
delights to gardeners, and one of
them is nurturing trees and shrubs.
Of course you'll water and fertilize
when necessary, and prune out broken
or tangled branches as required.
But the growing season is also a
good time to experiment. Take grafting,
for example. By grafting branches
of several different varieties of apple
onto one specimen, you can harvest all
your favourite varieties from a single tree!*

weeping eastern white pine (at left) and 'Dwarf Korean' lilac (at right)

Spring

What should I do to my shrub beds in the spring?

Lois ❖ Inspect the shrubs for winter damage, particularly damage by rodents. Prune out any damaged branches. Clean up any twigs, leaves, or other debris from around the base of the shrubs to reduce pest problems and make weeding easier. Cultivate or loosen the soil, being careful not to damage shallow-rooting shrubs such as azaleas, rhododendrons, and daphne. Top dress the base of plants (but not up against them) with compost. Fertilize early in the season, while the roots are actively growing. These steps will get your shrubs off to a strong, healthy start.

When should I unwrap cedars and other tender plants?

Lois ❖ As a rule, you can remove protective coverings from your tender plants as soon as the native trees are breaking bud. You may still see one or two hard frosts after this point, but they should cause little harm to the shrubs.

My trees are budding too early. What do I do?

Lois ❖ This is a common question, and unfortunately there's not much you can do. Humans simply can't control the weather. Most established trees, even if they sustain some damage from fluctuating temperatures, will recover on their own. The best you can do is keep your trees healthy and disease-free so they have a better chance of surviving whatever Mother Nature throws at them.

Jim ❖ The arrival of warmer weather signals trees and shrubs to end their winter dormancy and begin sending out flower and leaf buds. The warmer the weather, the quicker the emergence. Once the buds begin to swell, they can be injured by a sudden drop in temperature.

You can partially screen smaller shrubs from wind and sunlight, keeping them cooler and slowing the emergence of buds. Larger trees and shrubs, however, must fend for themselves.

We've had a heavy snowfall and some of my trees' buds have already emerged. What can I do?

Jim ❖ Snowfall won't injure the buds at all, provided the temperatures aren't too cold. If heavy, wet snow accumulates on the branches, however, it can break them. If possible, remove the snow by gently brushing or shaking it from the tree limbs.

'Minuet' weigela

Watering

How often should I water my tree?

Lois ❖ Water a newly transplanted tree several times per week for the first few weeks, until the root system becomes established. You seldom need to water mature trees, except during periods of drought. It's a good idea to water your trees during dry spells, to keep them lush, healthy, and less vulnerable to insects and diseases.

Jim ❖ A good rule is to provide 5 L of water per 30 cm of height or spread (whichever is greater) per week.

When is the best time of day to water?

Jim ❖ From a water-conservation perspective, it's best to apply water at the coolest time of day, because you'll lose less to evaporation. Apply coarse droplets that penetrate soil quickly, rather than broadcasting fine droplets into the air. The worst time to water is on hot, sunny, windy days; if you can, wait until evening to water.

Trees grow in hot and dry areas and nobody ever waters them. Why should I bother watering mine?

Lois ❖ If you take a good look at the trees you describe, you will likely notice a big difference in their size and overall health compared to a tree that is watered regularly. A beautiful, healthy tree is worth the time and trouble!

Jim ❖ Well-established trees are much better equipped to "find" water because they have large, extensive root systems. Some species of trees are also much better adapted to dry soils than others. However, all trees will be healthier if they aren't left in completely dry soil.

Drought tolerance doesn't imply that trees enjoy drought or that they will perform well under drought conditions. For instance, spruce trees can tolerate fairly dry soils, but if they become drought-stressed they will grow much more slowly and produce small, thin needles that are prone to attack by spider mites.

Fertilizing

How often should I fertilize my trees? What kind of fertilizer should I use?

Lois ❖ To answer this question properly I need to ask some questions of my own:

- What type of tree is it?
- How old is the tree?
- Is it newly transplanted or well established?
- What kind of soil is it growing in?

Try an all-purpose 20-20-20 fertilizer for deciduous trees and shrubs; 30-10-10 is better for evergreens.

Are trees heavy feeders? Do they require a lot of fertilizer to grow well?

Slow-release fertilizer provides a consistent supply of nutrients to shrubs and evergreens.

Jim ❖ Because they are so large, mature trees draw many minerals from the soil. However, they aren't heavy feeders on a year-to-year basis. Their root systems draw nutrients from a very large volume of soil, so they don't require much fertilizer to grow well.

Trees that have been newly transplanted in the spring will benefit from an application of fertilizer at the time of planting and once a month thereafter until the end of July. If you plant later in the growing season or even in late fall after the leaves have dropped, apply only one dose of fertilizer and continue your fertilizing program the next year.

On fertilizer packages, what do the three numbers represent?

Jim ❖ The numbers refer to the percentage by weight of nitrogen (the first number), phosphate (the middle number), and potash (the last number) in the fertilizer. Nitrogen is crucial for leaf growth, phosphates promote strong root development and flower formation, and potash aids in all-around plant health, fruit quality, and disease resistance. Keep in mind that all the nutrients interrelate and don't work independently. In other words, roots won't proliferate if phosphate is present without nitrogen.

What type of fertilizer and application method is best for trees and shrubs?

Lois ❖ Trees and shrubs can be fertilized a number of ways: stakes that you pound into the ground around the base of the plant, water-soluble fertilizer that you dilute and apply to the soil, and granules that you sprinkle on the soil and water in.

Jim ❖ Once your trees approach maturity, you don't need to fertilize as much or as often. Mature trees use a lot of nitrogen, so look for a fertilizer with a higher nitrogen content (the first number on the label). Don't overdo it, however. Too much nitrogen can cause excessively lush, weak growth that's more vulnerable to insects, disease, and winterkill. As a rule, you can apply nitrogen to the soil surface at a rate of 1 kg/100 m^2 annually.

'Makamik' crabapple

What is a root feeder, and how do I use it?

Jim ❖ A root feeder is a spike-like device about a metre long that injects fertilizer solution directly into the soil. You place a fertilizer cartridge into the reservoir at the top, and attach a garden hose. When you turn the water on, it dissolves the fertilizer and pushes the solution into the soil.

Insert the root feeder at six or eight spots around the drip line of the tree, to ensure even distribution of the fertilizer. Most of a tree's feeder roots are within 60 cm of the soil surface, so don't insert the root feeder too deep.

Can I use lawn fertilizer on my trees?

Jim ❖ You may not realize it, but tree roots absorb a portion of the lawn fertilizer whenever you apply it to the grass under your trees. Because of their high nitrogen content, lawn fertilizers can be excellent for trees, provided they don't contain herbicides like 2,4-D.

My friend doesn't use bone meal in her garden anymore because she's worried about mad-cow disease. Should I be worried too?

Jim ❖ I wouldn't worry. There's no compelling reason to consider bone meal unsafe, particularly in North America. We sell it at our greenhouse, and I don't hesitate to handle it myself. When mixed into the soil around trees and shrubs, bone meal provides an excellent slow-release source of phosphorus.

In 1996, England suffered a higher than usual incidence of Creutzfeldt-Jakob disease (CJD), a fatal brain disorder that normally strikes one person per million each year. Scientists believe the problem was linked to an epidemic of bovine spongiform encephalopathy (mad-cow disease) in English cattle. Some people fear that they risk exposure to mad-cow disease when they handle bone meal. However, to date no North American study has found any connection between CJD and bone meal.

Is it possible to over-fertilize? How can I tell I've done it?

Jim ❖ Yes, it is possible, particularly with newly transplanted trees. The smaller the tree and the smaller the root ball, the greater the risk. You normally apply the fertilizer directly to the planting hole, and when the hole is small, the fertilizer is concentrated. As the roots expand into a larger area, the danger of over-fertilizing is greatly reduced.

If a tree has been over-fertilized, the new growth will have brown edges—it will look almost burned. In severe cases, the burning may progress to the older growth. Flush the soil with water to help dilute the fertilizer.

What is the best method for fertilizing evergreens?

Jim ❖ On bare ground, use dry granular fertilizer or liquid feed. On grass-covered areas, use root feeders.

Can I grow trees organically?

Lois ❖ By all means, yes! You can certainly grow trees successfully without synthetic fertilizers or pest-control products. Virtually all of the naturally occurring trees in the world do just fine without any human intervention.

Pruning

Why should I prune my trees and shrubs?

Lois ❖ There are more than enough benefits to make it worth your while, not the least of which is a great-looking landscape.

Jim ❖ Here are a few of the benefits of pruning:

- Pruned plants look tidy, symmetrical, and proportional, and pruning encourages fruit and flowers.
- Well-pruned trees and shrubs produce fewer suckers.
- Pruning helps maintain plant health by removing diseased or insect-infected branches.
- Hazardous branches can damage houses, injure people, or contact electrical lines.
- If your home is obscured by greenery, it may be more vulnerable to criminals.

In general, when should I prune my trees?

Lois ❖ Pruning is a general term that we use to describe everything from deadheading to removing large limbs. It's best to prune large branches late in the dormant season. Prune in the late winter, just before spring growth starts. Of course, if a branch is broken or hazardous, it should be removed promptly, regardless of the time of year.

Jim ❖ Pruning in the summer, or while the tree is actively growing, can lead to several problems:

- Exposed cut ends are more vulnerable to disease and insect injury.
- If you remove too many leaves, you'll reduce your tree's ability to generate energy.

- It's harder to visualize the ultimate shape of your tree with leaves obscuring the view.

- In some regions, it is illegal to prune trees in the spring or summer due to insect problems.

There are, of course, exceptions to the rule. We recommend that birch and maple be pruned in late spring or early summer when they are fully leafed out, and most evergreens are best pruned in late spring, while the new growth is still soft.

Fall Pruning

Fall is a great time to prune. For one thing, trees are dormant in the fall and won't be unduly stressed when you start snipping branches. They're easier to get at, too, since most of the garden flowers are finished, so you don't have to worry about crushing them underfoot. More importantly, fall pruning removes a source of spring disease and insect problems—old, weak, or damaged branches.

proper pruning technique

There are a few rules, though. First and foremost, never try to prune a tree that's too big for you to handle. Without the proper training and equipment, pruning large trees can be dangerous. Do yourself a favour and call a certified arborist for the difficult or hazardous pruning jobs.

Never prune trees unless you've taken the time to learn how to make a proper cut. You'll do more harm than good, and there are plenty of good books with diagrams that show the difference between a healthy cut and one that can cause irreparable damage. I always recommend that beginners tackle only the small branches and leave the larger ones for the experts.

removing a portion of the candle

While you're pruning those small branches, make sure that you don't accidentally cut off any buds. Spring-flowering plants like azaleas, lilacs, and rhododendrons produce buds during the summer that lay dormant over winter for flower production the following spring. Obviously, if they are snipped off, no flowers will follow.

Shearing off a tree or shrub's canopy is a poor way to prune; doing so encourages the growth of weak, soft shoots. It's far better to thin instead. To thin, remove old, unproductive branches. This gives young branches room to spread out. Nanking cherries and dogwoods respond especially well to thinning; if they aren't thinned, they tend to become overgrown in just a few years.

Note that evergreens, unlike most trees, can be pruned while they are growing actively—that is, in late spring—to encourage bushy growth.

I can't prune my own trees anymore. A landscaping company will top my trees so that they don't need pruning for five years. Will this hurt my trees?

Lois ❖ Yes! The health of your trees (as well as their aesthetic value) may be compromised by such severe treatment. A slower program to get your trees to a manageable size would be much better.

Before you hire a landscape company, check that the work will be done by certified arborists. We've seen many examples of poor pruning that could have been avoided if a trained professional had been hired.

What is a certified arborist? Why should I hire one?

Lois ❖ A certified arborist is a specialist in tree care. To become certified, an arborist must have at least three years of work experience or equivalent education, and must pass a written exam. In addition, the arborist must accumulate a minimum number of formal classroom credits each year to retain certification. A certified arborist has the knowledge to solve difficult tree problems and to keep your trees in the best condition possible.

An example of pruning that has caused irreparable injury to the trees.

As a rule, how much growth should I remove from a tree's canopy?

Jim ❖ You shouldn't remove more than a third of a tree's overall growth at any one time. Heavy pruning can weaken a tree, leaving it vulnerable to disease and pests.

If you need to prune more than a third of the canopy, break your pruning schedule up into two or more sessions over a couple of years.

If a particular shrub flowers on "old wood" or last season's growth, when should I prune it?

Lois ❖ Trees or shrubs that bloom on old wood produce blooms on the previous season's growth and not on the current year's new shoots. Wait until the plant has finished flowering, in the late spring or early summer.

Jim ❖ You can prune the shrub in the early spring, along with the rest of your trees and shrubs without affecting the shrub's health. However, you risk removing flowerbuds. Pruning after the blooming period is best.

Why can't I prune my trees and shrubs when they are growing actively?

Jim ❖ For most trees and shrubs, pruning while they are growing actively increases the chance of insect or disease damage, because the cut ends will be exposed when the pests are abundant. Dormant pruning allows a plant to redirect growth, which doesn't happen when a tree is fully leafed out. Pruning out fully leafed limbs also reduces a tree's ability to produce food.

You can trim many plants, such as hedges and fast-growing shrubs, when they are not dormant.

When is the best time to prune evergreens?

Lois ❖ The general rule is to prune evergreens while they are actively growing or while the new growth is still soft.

Jim ❖ Most evergreens need very little pruning. However, if you're after thick, dense-looking trees, you can do some minor pruning. Pinch off as many as a third of the "candles," or tips, while they are elongating; don't prune back into old growth. On junipers, yews, hemlock, and false cypress, you can trim the new growth after it has emerged in spring but before it has started to harden and mature in mid to late summer.

How often should I prune my cotoneaster or alpine currant hedge?

Jim ❖ Cotoneaster and alpine currant hedges need to be pruned regularly to maintain a nice shape. These plants grow very quickly during the long, warm days of summer, so you may have to trim weekly.

If you leave it too long, you'll have to cut the hedge back severely, leaving the plants looking sparse for quite a while. The newly exposed leaves also sunburn easily.

What can I do to keep my shrubs tidy?

Lois ❖ Keep your secateurs handy and in good condition. If your shrubs are gangly, chances are they haven't been pruned properly or frequently.

People often leave pruning until the tree or shrub is out of control, and at that point, the pruning becomes butchering. Proper pruning is really training—redirecting growth and eliminating broken or diseased branches as soon as they appear. Carry the secateurs out to the garden so that you'll be ready to tackle any problem.

Serious pruning should be kept to specific times of the year, but no season is off limits for minor snipping and training.

If I prune my flowering shrub too severely in the early spring, will it look bad all summer?

Lois ❖ It depends on the extent of the damage. It can easily take a season or two for a severely pruned shrub to recover fully, and it may not bloom for that length of time.

'Gold Drop' potentilla

Should I cut my trees back once they stop blooming? Will it hurt them?

Jim ❖ Don't cut trees back. Your tree will be healthier if you perform selective pruning at the right time of year. You can remove withered flowers without causing any harm, but "shaving" the plant creates weak, unattractive sucker growth.

I've heard that you should prune to an outward-facing bud, but I'm not sure what that means.

Jim ❖ On most trees and shrubs, buds can arise on various spots on the branches. Ideally, a plant is healthiest and most aesthetically pleasing if it is "opened up" to allow for good sunlight penetration and air movement.

To achieve this, you should prune your branches just above a bud that is facing the outside of the plant (that is, away from its centre). If you prune down to an inward-facing bud, you'll end up with a branch that grows inward towards the centre of the plant.

Why shouldn't I prune with dull shears or a carpenter's saw?

Jim ❖ Dull shears are not only difficult to use but also can cause injury to the shrub or tree. Dull shears leave tattered stubs that don't heal properly.

A carpenter's saw tends to jam when pruning because the teeth aren't designed for wet wood. It is also too long and straight for tight spaces. A pruning saw has a shorter, curved blade, reducing the danger of injuring other branches while pruning.

how to prune a large branch

Make a cut on the underside of the branch approximately one-third to one-half of the way through the branch.

Make the top cut slightly outside—towards the branch end—of the bottom cut. Continue cutting until you are through the branch.

After the pre-cut, you have a short stub that is easier to remove.

The final cut should be clean, straight, and always to the outside of the branch bark ridge.

The Well-Stocked Toolshed

When I stock up on gardening gear, I always follow one cardinal rule: buy durable, high-quality tools, even when they're more expensive. A low price is no bargain if you end up throwing away a broken tool just months after you buy it. Here are some tools I consider essential.

- A sturdy **water wand** with a flood nozzle provides a gentle, high-volume shower of droplets and delivers a good soaking without bowling plants over.
- A Haws **watering can** is made of durable galvanized steel, rests perfectly balanced in your hand, and has a long spout to make reaching much easier.
- A **high-quality rubber hose** is a must. Vinyl hoses crack and are hard to handle.
- A **stirrup hoe** sweeps through the soil to cut weed seedlings without disturbing your shrubs or moving the soil.
- A **soil scoop**, a hand tool with a large serrated edge and a pointed tip, is great for digging and mixing soil.
- **Hose-end spray applicators** for pest-control and fertilizer products allow you to meter out chemicals accurately.
- A good-quality set of **secateurs (pruners)**— you cannot grow healthy trees and shrubs without them! Clean them thoroughly after each job, and apply a few drops of oil to the blades regularly.
- A **pruning saw** with a shorter, curved blade is best for effective pruning.

Keep your tools in a clean, dry location, so they'll always be ready to handle any gardening task.

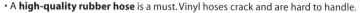

How should I clean my pruners after trimming black knot or fireblight off my trees?

Lois ❖ Cleaning your pruners between cuts is a good all-around practice. Two products work well: bleach (sodium hypochlorite) and ethyl alcohol (ethanol). Dip the pruners in the solution after each cut to avoid spreading disease.

Jim ❖ Bleach eats into metal, so don't leave your pruners in the bleach solution for any length of time. After the job is done, apply a lightweight oil to the blades to prevent rust damage.

Use a ten-percent bleach solution (one part household bleach to nine parts water) or a seventy-percent ethanol solution.

How can I prune branches that are 4 cm in diameter and 3 m above the ground?

Jim ❖ A pole pruner is your best bet. For a branch that size, you'll need the sawblade attachment. Keep in mind that a 4-cm branch can be dangerous when it falls. Consider hiring a certified arborist.

'Ramapo' rhododendron

Tatarian maple

My maple tree is 15 m tall and growing into a power line. Can I cut it back to 10 m?

Lois ❖ Leave this job to a professional. Hire a certified arborist.

Jim ❖ It's extremely dangerous to prune trees anywhere near a power line. You also risk severely injuring a tree if you cut it back that drastically, potentially transforming it into a hazardous tree in the future.

I'm building a deck. Can I make room for it by cutting part of the bark off one side of my large tree?

Lois ❖ That's like cutting off your own flesh to fit a smaller pair of pants! Bark is a living, necessary part of a tree, not unlike human skin. Don't remove it!

Jim ❖ No, for a couple of reasons. First, removing bark exposes the trunk to pest attack. The tree could weaken and become a hazard. Second, even with the bark removed, the tree trunk will continue to expand in girth and will eventually outgrow its allotted space.

Keeping Trees and Shrubs Healthy

Is it all right to make a raised bed around an already-established tree?

Lois ❖ No. If you add a thick layer of soil, you will deprive the roots of oxygen and may seriously injure the tree.

Jim ❖ Most tree roots are found in the top metre of soil. Feeder roots (the very fine roots) grow in the top 30 cm. Roots need moisture, nutrients, and oxygen to thrive. If the oxygen level drops below three percent of the soil volume, growth essentially stops.

How can I tell if a tree should be staked?

Lois ❖ We generally recommend that you stake any newly planted tree two metres or taller.

Jim ❖ Well-rooted trees with a good "root-to-shoot" ratio seldom require staking. Tall, thin deciduous trees are at greater risk. Stake them on two or three sides. Nylon ropes secured to well-anchored wooden stakes are inexpensive and effective. Cover the rope with a protective collar wherever it touches the tree, and allow several inches of "play" at the top; otherwise the rubbing can severely damage the branches and trunk. Play is important because the tree's movement will encourage proper root development. One full growing season is generally long enough for a tree to become properly anchored.

I covered my shrubs with plastic to protect them while I sprayed Roundup. When can I uncover them?

Jim ❖ You can uncover them as soon as the Roundup solution is dry. Roundup (glyphosate) is immobilized quickly after it touches the soil, so it won't hurt your shrubs after the application.

Should I cultivate around my shrubs?

Lois ❖ Yes, but do it lightly and use a stirrup hoe. If you till too deeply, you'll injure the feeder roots, especially on shallow-rooting shrubs like azalea, rhododendron, and daphne.

Jim ❖ Over time, the soil in your shrub beds settles and may become compacted. Cultivating around shrubs reduces weed competition.

Should I use weed barrier on my shrubs?

Lois ❖ Weed barriers, properly installed and maintained, can reduce the amount of time you spend hunched over your shrub beds.

Jim ❖ Use caution. Weed barriers prevent many weeds from emerging, but they also intercept water and reduce the movement of oxygen into the soil. Some people also cover the barrier with a thick mulch, which further hinders the movement of water and oxygen. If you use a weed barrier, ensure that the roots get enough water, and keep mulching to a maximum of 3 cm.

Compact Trees

Customers often ask us to recommend trees small enough to fit into an urban landscape. Many have battled with a tree that has overgrown its site, its branches endangering power lines, its roots invading flowerbeds. But the good news is that there are plenty of compact choices with shorter heights, narrower spreads, and more balanced forms than typical trees.

Before you choose a compact tree, try to get a good idea of how large you'd like it to be at maturity. You should also take into account how much sunlight is available, what your soil conditions are, and what function you would like your tree to accomplish—will it provide shade, screen off unpleasant views, fit in with an existing theme? Do you want fall colour, or an evergreen? By knowing these things before you head to the nursery, you stand a much better chance of finding a plant that suits your garden.

Siberian columnar crabapple

These are some of our favourite compact trees. Some of the varieties mentioned here are naturally compact, while others are the results of hybridization programs. All are great choices for gardeners looking for big beauty in a small package. No matter if your size choice is restricted by space or design constraints, there are many varieties that should meet your needs.

Fast-growing and disease-resistant, 'Assiniboine' and 'Prairie Sky' poplars are both great choices for smaller yards. Also check out 'Bailey's Schubert' chokecherry, 'Snowbird' or 'Toba' hawthorn, 'Advance' mayday, or 'Columnar European' mountain ash.

Ornamental fruit trees provide an awesome spring showing of blooms, attractive small fruits, and often great fall colour. 'Mountain Frost' pear and 'Rosy Glo' or 'Siberian Columnar' crabapples are terrific compact ornamental fruits.

You don't have to have a huge amount of space to enjoy fresh fruit from your own tree. Dwarf apple trees have normal-sized fruits of exactly the same variety as full-sized trees, but with more manageable yields. Look for dwarf 'Norland,' 'Norkent,' 'Fall Red,' 'Goodland,' and 'September Ruby.'

Columnar evergreens are always popular, and 'Brandon,' 'Degroot's Spire,' and 'Holmstrup' cedars offer very narrow columnar forms in a variety of heights. Junipers such as 'Blue Arrow,' 'Cologreen,' and 'Grey Gleam' or spruces like 'Cupress,' 'Dwarf Serbian,' and 'Iseli Columnar Blue' are varieties worth trying.

'Degroot's Spire' cedar

Growing in Containers

Can I grow trees in a large container?

Lois ❖ Customers often confuse containers with planters that are really raised beds. The difference is that a container completely contains or holds the plant's roots and soil. A raised bed is open at the bottom and allows much more latitude in what can be planted in it, as the plants' roots can penetrate the soil beneath the bed.

A container is relative to the size of tree you are attempting to grow in it. The larger the tree, the more room for soil and roots it requires. Some smaller trees and shrubs will do just fine in containers if properly cared for. But many trees won't do well because they are too large or too sensitive to winter injury.

Jim ❖ Plants grown in containers have a greater tendency to dry out or be damaged by winter cold. Roots in containers can't obtain moisture from as great a soil volume as an in-ground tree and are exposed to much colder temperatures because they aren't insulated by the ground. Trees in containers tend to be somewhat stunted, simply because there is less room for the roots to grow.

How big does a container have to be to overwinter shrubs?

Lois ❖ The bigger, the better. Container-grown species typically survive better in areas with mild winters.

Jim ❖ A large soil volume insulates roots much better than a small soil volume. Some species are also more cold tolerant than others and will do well in smaller containers.

Can I grow a tree in a pot on my deck or balcony during the summer?

Lois ❖ During the summer, small trees and shrubs will grow well in pots, provided that you pay close attention to watering.

Jim ❖ Many likely won't survive the winter in containers, however, because their roots will be exposed to low temperatures. Those that do survive will likely outgrow even fairly large pots in a few seasons. If you're considering growing a tree in a pot, choose a dwarf variety, and if you're in an area with harsh, cold winters, treat it as an annual.

How often should I water a tree in a container?

Lois ❖ Water small containers every other day; large containers may need only weekly watering. Water more often during hot spells, and less often in cool weather.

Jim ❖ Container-grown trees can only draw moisture from the soil in their containers. The smaller the container, the more often you'll have to water. If the top 2 cm of soil feels dry, it's time to water.

Species also influences water demand. Some trees and shrubs are water hogs, while others use their moisture more efficiently.

Fall Clean-Up

The shorter, cooler days of autumn act as a signal to many of the most notorious garden pests. Make no mistake: they're not leaving your yard for greener pastures. They're waiting for winter to pass so they can return to feed on your plants next summer.

Simply raking up leaves and debris in the yard can substantially reduce the impact of many pest problems. Ideally, your yard should be pristine before a lasting snowfall, but realistically, few of us are ever that lucky or ambitious. Just do your best!

Apple scab, the disease that causes ugly brown lesions on apple leaves and fruits, overwinters comfortably on apple leaf debris left on the lawn. Be sure to rake up and compost apple leaves.

Two excellent treatments for many trees and shrubs are dormant oil and lime-sulphur spray. Dormant oil can be sprayed on trunks and branches to destroy many overwintering pests, such as mites and aphid eggs. Lime-sulphur spray is a combination of lime and sulphur that's used to control orchard pests. Ensure that the products penetrate the cracks and crevices where overwintering pests hide. Apply them while temperatures are still above freezing to trees and shrubs that have lost all of their leaves.

Damp, matted leaves and grass clippings provide an ideal environment for snow mould, the white, fuzzy growth that attacks grass in the spring. Remove leaves and grass thatch to reduce the incidence of snow mould.

Galvanized wire meshes or plastic tree guards placed around trunks protect trees against hungry animals, like rodents and deer.

Fall clean-up can involve a good deal of work. But by completing these chores in autumn, you can look forward to a spring with fewer unwanted visitors.

Winter

How can I keep my trees from cracking over the winter?

Jim ❖ Tree trunks split when they undergo rapid freezing and thawing. Some species are more prone than others.

Trees have fewer problems if their trunks are protected from direct sunlight. If your trees are cracking, try providing some screening. You can also use trunk wraps on small trees.

What can I do to protect my tender shrubs for the winter?

Lois ❖ First, ensure that you keep your plants healthy during the growing season. Healthy plants build up higher energy reserves, enabling them to endure winter much more easily.

Regular watering, plus late-season watering (two weeks before freeze up), aids winter survival. Mulching can also help tremendously. Peat moss, loose leaves, and snow are all excellent insulators.

Jim ❖ Placement is also important: a yard usually has a few places that offer some protection to tender shrubs. A spot that is screened from the prevailing wind or against the foundation is a good choice.

Can I bring my tender shrubs inside during the winter?

Jim ❖ When you bring plants inside during the winter, the enemy becomes the heat rather than cold. A warm environment will cause some species to begin growing. With the low light levels inside your home, a growing plant quickly burns up its energy reserves and often dies.

Most temperate-region plants must undergo winter chilling to complete their life cycle. Unless they accumulate enough hours of cold during the winter, they may fail to leaf out or flower in the spring. If you can keep the temperature consistently within a few degrees of freezing, the trees will do fine inside—but this isn't practical or even possible in most homes.

That said, some species can do fairly well in consistently cool garages (around the freezing mark). Check with your local garden centre.

Siberian dogwood

How do I know which shrubs to mulch?

Lois ❖ You can eliminate many of them simply because they're too big. With smaller shrubs, you can decide whether or not to mulch based on their hardiness. You should mulch small tender or borderline-hardy shrubs every fall.

Jim ❖ Make a note when purchasing shrubs from a nursery of which ones may be tender or out-of-zone plants. You might also consider purchasing a good reference book that will give you zone information, as well as other valuable advice.

How do I mulch?

Lois ❖ Your mulch should be loose, dry, and free of pests (weeds, insects, and disease). Use peat moss, dry, clean leaves, or even snow when it's available. You can also use straw, provided it's weed-free. Pile the mulch over the plants. Never pack it down or you'll reduce its insulation value. Use a light layer of soil to hold the mulch in place. Watch for mice!

Jim ❖ If you use leaves, they should be thick and coarse so they don't compact when they get wet. Compacted leaves can form a barrier that will take a long time to thaw in the spring and may even suffocate the plant. Shred the leaves, or use peat moss or compost.

CHAPTER 5 ❀
ENJOYING TREES AND SHRUBS

Everyone likes to bring a little of the beauty of the forest home. When I was younger, I used to collect pussy willows from the river valley and put them in a vase. These days I'm more conscious of the environmental impact of such collecting, so I harvest only from my own yard. Today, my favourite floral arrangements often include woody plants such as ilex, curly willow, and forsythia.

Can I use the blossoms from my trees and shrubs for cutflowers?

Lois ❖ Yes! Lilacs are a great example of a flower that is excellent both outdoors and indoors. As a rule, pick flowers at the tighter flower-bud stage to increase longevity in the vase.

Jim ❖ To help your flowers last longer, treat them as you would any cutflowers. Here are some more tips to help flowers last longer:

- Bacterial infection can cause your blooms to wilt. To prevent infection, rinse your vase thoroughly with a bleach solution to sterilize it, then rinse it again with plain water to remove the bleach residue.

- Before putting the flowers in your vase, re-cut the stems.

- Always cut the stems underwater to avoid embolisms (trapped air bubbles that prevent water flow within the stems).

- Cut the stems at a 45° angle. This exposes a greater surface area to the water and keeps the ends off the bottom of the vase, allowing the stems to draw water more easily. Sometimes smashing the cut ends of woody stems with a hammer will increase water uptake.

- Cut off any foliage that will be below the waterline to prevent rotting.

- Add floral preservative, to supply sugar and prevent bacterial growth.

- Keep your vase in a cool location, away from direct sunlight.

- Change the water in the container frequently.

best trees & shrubs for floral arrangements

alder (seedheads)
boxwood (foliage)
cedar (foliage)
daphne
dogwood
golden plume elder
forsythia
Harry Lauder's
    walking stick
holly
lilac
'Diabolo' ninebark
Russian almond
sandcherry
willow

Harry Lauder's walking stick

I'd like to add some foliage to my hand-picked bouquets. Are there any shrubs that could provide suitable foliage?

Lois ❖ Euonymus and holly, with their glossy leaves, are excellent choices for bouquets. They are used extensively by florists.

Jim ❖ Taking a few branches for bouquets does no harm to these shrubs, provided, of course, that you don't prune out too much.

Foliage Shrubs

Most novice gardeners tend to fill their garden oasis with a riot of beautiful blooming but short-lived plants. Gardeners who have been playing the game a little longer often take a closer look at what's available in nurseries today and gravitate toward woody plants with unusual foliage.

'Emerald Mound' honeysuckle

Some claim that foliage is boring. Not at all! A great foliage shrub will add interest to your garden for a long stretch of the season, as well as texture and large blocks of colour—all important elements in good landscape design. Foliage shrubs can also serve as a background that makes those beloved blooming plants stand out even more.

'Madonna' elder

'Diabolo' ninebark is a relatively new foliage shrub from Europe. Its dark stems support deep purple/burgundy leaves with fuchsia buds opening to soft-pink blooms in spring. This shrub is outstanding on its own and also pairs up nicely with gold-toned foliage shrubs such as the lacy-leafed 'Golden Plume' elder for a long-lived show of colour and texture. Or try combining 'Diabolo' with the soft-pink 'Morden Blush' rose—the dark leaves of the ninebark make the roses pop right out at you.

Another underused new introduction, cutleaf stephanandra has finely textured foliage on long, arching stems that tend to root wherever they touch the soil. This shrub is gorgeous when it winds around rocks or when plopped in front of an 'Emerald Mound' honeysuckle—or, for that matter, any one of the old favourite variegated dogwoods.

Another new introduction, 'Silver and Gold' dogwood is quite striking with its variegated foliage and bright-yellow twigs. Perfect for adding interest to a winter landscape! If you love the look of variegated dogwoods, consider trying 'Madonna' elder, 'Emerald 'n Gold' euonymus, or 'Carol Mackie' daphne.

My friend cuts branches off her shrubs in late winter and forces them to bloom indoors. How do I do this?

Lois ❖ This is a wonderful way to treat yourself to a preview of spring! In late winter, snip off a few branches. Bring them inside, peel off the bottom couple of inches of bark, and smash the stem ends with a hammer to increase water uptake. Put the stems immediately into a vase of warm water and place them in a warm, sunny spot to break their dormancy. Depending on the type of stems, expect flower buds to open within one to four weeks.

Jim ❖ Some of the best varieties for forcing include cherry, double-flowering plum, forsythia, lilac, plum, Russian almond, and sandcherry.

Can I cut and use my shrub's branches for flower arrangements or will that damage my shrub?

Lois ❖ You certainly can! Many floral designers use branches to add texture, shape, colour, and height to arrangements. Pussy willows are a familiar choice, but you can also try dogwood, ninebark, elders, and many others. Just don't get too enthusiastic and cut off too many. Leave a few branches for the shrub!

How can I make my shrubs flower longer and more profusely?

Jim ❖ I'm afraid that the duration of flowering depends more on Mother Nature than on you. A shrub's natural blooming time may be three weeks long. Individual blooms last longer during cool weather, while hot temperatures accelerate the demise of flowers. You can have some effect on the number of blooms you get by keeping the shrub healthy and pruning appropriately.

How does statuary add to my garden? What's a gazing globe?

Lois ❖ Statuary complements your garden much like art complements the interior of your home (and, like art, is just as much a matter of personal taste!). Statuary is enjoying a revival as gardeners focus on all aspects of landscaping.

A gazing globe is a reflective glass sphere available in many colours. Check your local garden centre for availability.

What can I use to overwinter statuary? Mine sometimes cracks over the winter.

Lois ❖ Water accumulates in cracks and expands as it freezes. The freezing and thawing cycle often repeats several times over the course of a winter. This can gradually make a tiny crack larger and larger, eventually breaking the statue.

Jim ❖ To prevent this, simply cover your statuary with black plastic when you clean up your garden in the fall. If the piece isn't too large, you can move it into a shed or garage. Statuary can also be resealed in the fall. Most statuary companies have their own resealing products; check with your local garden centre.

How can I use trees and shrubs to attract birds to my yard?

Lois ❖ Many people have birdfeeders in their yards in winter, but you can also grow trees and shrubs to provide food for birds year-round. If your plants provide shelter as well as food, birds will be more likely to make your yard their home. A mixture of deciduous and evergreen trees and shrubs attracts many different birds, providing them with protective cover as well as nesting sites.

best trees and shrubs for attracting birds

arrowwood
birch
cedar
cherry prinsepia
chokecherry (except 'Autumn Magic')
cotoneaster
American highbush cranberry
Wentworth cranberry
Adams elder
red-berried elder
fir
juniper
mayday
mountain ash
Nanking cherry
nannyberry
pincherry
pine
roses
seviceberry
spruce
wayfaring tree

Nanking cherry

I'd like to try some topiary in my yard. How do I begin?

Lois ❖ Topiary forms are a wonderful feature in a landscape and can be a lot of fun to try. Start with something easy to grow and choose a simple topiary form. Remember that every cut or prune you make will, over time, contribute to the final shape.

Jim ❖ Topiary is the selective pruning and shaping of a plant to a form that is not its natural shape. This training usually starts with young plants and takes many years. Once you achieve the effect you're looking for, you have to keep working to maintain it. Formal gardens, particularly in Europe, are famous for their fantastically shaped hedges and features.

Junipers, particularly the 'Mint Julep' and 'Seagreen' varieties, are among the more popular evergreens used for topiary. For deciduous topiary trees, choose a multi-stemmed variety such as amur maple, and train it to a single-stemmed form. You can also try a number of shrubs, including lilacs, arctic willow, ninebarks, and hedging plants like cotoneaster and alpine currant.

Beautifully Trained Trees

Training a tree involves intensive, ongoing work. But a shapely tree attracts attention like no other feature, and the challenge can be immensely rewarding. Once you've mastered the basics of pruning, you're ready to try creating your own living art. Here are some of the most common trained forms.

Juniperus wiltoni

'Seagreen' juniper pompon

Scotch pine bonsai

living-art juniper

- **Topiary:** Also know as "sculptured" trees, topiary forms can be as simple or complex as the creator desires. Yews, spruce, and broadleaf evergreens like laurels and boxwoods are particularly suited to this art form.

- **Bonsai:** Many people associate bonsai with small shrubs, but larger plants can also be trained in the traditional Japanese manner. Flowering plants can be particularly striking in this form.

- **Espalier:** Espaliers are two-dimensional forms. The branches are trained to grow horizontally along a fence or wall to create pictures such as pyramids and diamonds.

- **Cordon:** A cordon, a variation of the espalier, is a trained form often used with fruit trees. The branches are trained to follow a vertical or oblique pattern.

- **Oriental Pompon:** Pompons usually appear as upright, multi-branched forms, each branch topped with a sphere of foliage. Pompons are most common on evergreens.

- **Spirals:** Spirals are trees trained to grow in the form of a corkscrew. They make excellent frames for the entrance to a garden or driveway. Junipers and cedars are the most common trees used for spirals.

- **Serpentine:** Serpentine forms have an upright, snake-like main stem with smaller branches hanging or weeping from it. Birch and larch trees are often used for serpentines.

- **Dautsugi:** In this form, two or more plant cultivars are grafted onto a single rootstock. For example, a globe spruce may be grafted to a weeping Norway for a striking combination of upright and weeping branches.

formed golden pfitzer

amur maackia

What is a living fence, and how can I grow one?

Lois ❖ A living fence is simply a line of shrubs or trees planted to form a solid barrier. Hedging is an example, as are windrows and screens.

A living fence adds a wonderful backdrop to your yard, one that changes with the seasons and may even bloom (if, for example, you've planted lilacs). It also makes your yard more private. We've seen living arbours, gazebos, and even garden benches!

Jim ❖ Choose a plant that meets your needs for height and width, keeping in mind other growth characteristics like density, suckering habit, watering, and pruning. Then plant and space your choice in the length and width you require. You may find it easier to dig and prepare a single trench to plant in, rather than a multitude of single holes for individual plants. Allow the trees or shrubs to grow into a natural form, or sculpt to a more manicured form.

What is a good tree to grow near my deck?

Lois ❖ A good choice is a tidy tree: one that doesn't drop fruit or seeds or drip sap. Some of our favourites include Morden hawthorn, linden, amur maackia, and many of the maples.

Jim ❖ How much space do you have? Would you prefer a single or multi-stemmed tree? Do you want to sit under a canopy of dappled or dense shade? Figure out what you want and choose a tree that suits your needs.

My mountain ash tree has a bumper crop of berries this year. Can I use them for jam or wine?

Lois ❖ Mountain ash berries have a long history of culinary use. The varieties have been used for not only jams and jellies but also as ketchup, liqueurs, syrup, vinegar, dried like prunes, and even as a coffee substitute! The orange berries of Russian mountain ash in particular are said to be sweet and high in vitamin C.

Can I make jelly from pincherry fruit?

Lois ❖ I have a love-hate relationship with pincherries. In my opinion, pincherries produce the best-tasting jelly of any fruit. But because the fruits are so tiny, it takes hours to harvest enough to make a single jar of jelly!

Are the apples on my ornamental crabapple edible?

Lois ❖ Yes. Crabapples are generally small and quite tart, but they're edible and good for making jellies or wine.

What are the official trees for each province and territory?

Lois ❖ This is a wonderful question! What better way to celebrate the diversity of Canada than by planting the emblematic trees in your garden.

- British Columbia: western red cedar, *Thuja plicata*
- Alberta: lodgepole pine, *Pinus contorta*
- Saskatchewan: paper birch, *Betula papyrifera*
- Manitoba: white spruce, *Picea glauca*
- Ontario: eastern white pine, *Pinus strobus*
- Quebec: yellow birch, *Betula alleghaniensis*
- New Brunswick: balsam fir, *Abies balsamea*
- Prince Edward Island: northern red oak, *Quercus rubra*
- Nova Scotia: red spruce, *Picea rubens*
- Newfoundland and Labrador: black spruce, *Picea mariana*
- Yukon: quaking aspen, *Populus tremuloides*
- Northwest Territories: jack pine, *Pinus banksiana*
- Nunavut: None named to date.

I find it interesting that eight out of twelve official trees are evergreens.

Jim ❖ Each US state also has an official tree. Here are a few examples:

- Alaska: Sitka spruce, *Picea sitchensis*
- California: redwood, *Sequoia sempervirens*
- Colorado: blue spruce, *Picea pungens*
- Idaho: western white pine, *Pinus monticola*
- Maine: eastern white pine, *Pinus strobus*
- Michigan: eastern white pine, *Pinus strobus*
- Montana: ponderosa pine, *Pinus ponderosa*
- New York: sugar maple, *Acer saccharum*
- North Dakota: American elm, *Ulmus americana*
- Oregon: douglas-fir, *Pseudotsuga menziesii*
- South Dakota: white spruce, *Picea glauca*
- Utah: blue spruce, *Picea pungens*
- Vermont: sugar maple, *Acer saccharum*
- Washington: western hemlock, *Tsuga heterophylla*

CHAPTER 6 ❧
TROUBLESHOOTING

The key to dealing with many tree and shrub problems is to learn all you can about the nature of the difficulty. Cedar-apple rust creates a foreboding orange horn on cedar and apple trees, and it certainly fascinated me the first time I saw it. But once I did some research into the life cycle of the organism, it became far easier to understand how it affects a tree's health— and how to prevent its spread.

'Gold Prince' euonymus

What is the difference between a sucker and a water sprout?

Lois ❖ A sucker comes from the base of a tree, near the soil line, while a water sprout emerges from the trunk or a branch, higher up the tree.

Jim ❖ A flush of suckers or water sprouts often indicates that the tree is stressed by damage to roots or excessive pruning.

How do I keep quackgrass from growing between my shrubs?

Lois ❖ The simplest solution is to eliminate the quackgrass before you plant and then make sure it doesn't have a chance to get re-established.

If you have the opportunity, spray the quackgrass with glyphosate when it is 15 cm high or taller. The quackgrass will die in ten days to two weeks. Keep your eye open for any remaining green blades, and re-spray as necessary. Once the bed is clear, plant your shrubs. You may also find a weed barrier or a thick mulch effective in stopping quackgrass from starting from seed.

Jim ❖ It's hard to get rid of quackgrass once it starts growing through the shrubs. Fortunately, most shrubs compete well and can fend off the quack grass.

Glyphosate works well, but use it only in spots where there's no risk of hitting the shrubs. Some of our customers have gone as far as to paint it on each blade of grass with a cotton swab.

Why have the leaves on one branch of my variegated-leafed euonymus turned green?

Jim ❖ Variegation is the result of cells that mutated at one time and were deliberately propagated by a grower to create a variegated variety. Sometimes the mutation isn't stable, and the plant reverts back to its parent colour. The stability of a variegated plant depends on where in the leaf tissue the original mutation occurred. Further, a single bud may not contain the mutated cells, and the bud will grow into an entire branch of green leaves.

Why aren't my flowering shrubs flowering this year?

Jim ❖ There are several possible causes:

- Immature shrubs sometimes take a few years to blossom.
- The shrubs may not be getting enough sunlight. If the light energy is too low, the plants won't produce blooms. Light levels may now be reduced because surrounding trees or other shrubs have grown up.
- You may have inadvertently removed the flower buds while pruning.
- The buds may have been injured by cold winter weather. Flower buds are more sensitive than leaf buds, so a brutal cold snap may wipe out the blossoms while leaving the leaves intact. For example, the leaf buds on a double-flowering plum will survive -40°C, but the flower buds won't.
- The shrub may have insect or disease problems.

What causes browning on evergreens?

Lois ❖ There are many reasons for an evergreen to turn brown, but most often this happens when the needles aren't getting enough water. Water your evergreens heavily once per week during the growing season. Newly transplanted trees are particularly vulnerable because their root systems aren't well established. Water them two or three times a week for the first few weeks.

Needles can also dry out and turn brown in winter. When the soil freezes, the roots can't replace the water lost from the needles. The problem is worst during sunny, mild, and windy winters. You can reduce winter browning by watering your evergreens heavily in the late fall.

Jim ❖ Spray-on antidesiccants like Wiltpruf help reduce moisture loss in winter, although they're not a cure-all. Brown needles can also be caused by insect injury, herbicides, and spilled chemicals such as gasoline.

Moss is growing on my tree! What should I do?

Lois ❖ Don't do anything. The moss (or, in many cases, lichens) causes no harm to the tree. Mosses are nearly impossible to control, so your best bet is just to learn to appreciate them.

Jim ❖ When the weather is moist and cool, lichens and mosses flourish. Conversely, hot, dry weather suspends their growth.

What does "chilling requirement" mean?

Jim ❖ Chilling requirement refers to the minimum number of hours of cool temperatures required before a seed or plant will grow or fruit. Chilling requirement is a plant adaptation to winter in cool or cold climates. If the plant didn't have a chilling requirement, it would start to grow in the middle of a winter warm spell, only to be injured when the weather turned cold again. With a minimum number of hours of cold required, there's an excellent chance the plant will not attempt to grow until well after the danger of a killing frost has passed.

Many temperate plants such as apples and peaches don't grow well in warm winter climates because their chilling requirements aren't met. The winters are too mild for them to grow properly.

How do I get rid of fireblight?

Jim ❖ Fireblight is a highly infectious disease of several species of trees and shrubs. It is the most devastating bacterial disease of apple, mountain ash, and members of the genus *Prunus*. There are several precautions you can take against fireblight:

- Plant fireblight-resistant varieties. Some apple varieties are much more resistant than others.

- Avoid pruning trees when the fireblight bacteria are abundant (i.e., spring and summer).

- Inspect plants weekly and remove visible lesions or infected branches. Prune down at least 20 cm, then destroy the infected branches. Do not leave them in your yard or attempt to chip them and use them for mulch.

- Disinfect pruning tools with bleach or ethanol between cuts to prevent spreading the disease.

What are mychorrizal fungi? Do I need them?

Jim ❖ Mychorrizal fungi are fungi that invade the roots of many plants. In most cases, this invasion is good for both the plant and the fungi. The fungi extract nutrients from the roots, but they also search for nutrients like phosphorus and zinc for the plant. Thus, the relationship is symbiotic, or mutually beneficial. Mychorrizal fungi exist in many soils naturally, but some soils are virtually devoid of them. In these cases, there are commercial products containing mychorrizal fungi that you can add to the soil at planting time; check with your local garden centre.

What are the large bumps on my tree trunk?

Lois ❖ They could be burls. Burls are simply large, knobby growths, quite common on many species of trees, including pines. The exact cause isn't known, but in some cases it could be the result of infection.

Jim ❖ Burls can also be regions where dormant buds predominate. If a tree is severely pruned or damaged, shoots will emerge from these buds.

I have heavy clay soil. Does putting gravel in the bottom of my planting hole increase drainage?

Jim ❖ No. In fact, gravel makes drainage worse. The gravel intercepts the movement of water from the soil above to the soil below. It's far better to incorporate organic matter into the entire area before planting, rather than planting your tree or shrub into heavy clay soil.

golden plume elder

Injuries

My tree was ravaged by hail. Will it recover?

Lois ❖ Hail rarely causes any long-term damage to trees. During the spring and summer, trees can replace destroyed leaves fairly quickly. Your tree should be back to normal in a few weeks.

Jim ❖ Severe storms can cause less obvious damage, too. Even if your trees haven't been shredded by hail, you may want to check for limbs broken or weakened by high winds.

A large crack developed in the trunk of my tree over winter. What can I do? Will my tree die?

Jim ❖ There are many methods for repairing trees, but unless you have advanced tree-care knowledge, call an arborist for assistance.

Cabling and bracing are commonly used to repair injuries. Cable is used in combination with bolts or lag screws to support weak or damaged limbs. Bracing can be used to support weak branches, to bind split crotches or trunks, and to stop limbs from rubbing; cavities, such as a large crack, may also be braced. However, if the injury is severe, it may be best to replace the tree.

How do I fix a gouge in my tree trunk?

Jim ❖ Clean up the tattered bark with a knife. This eliminates hiding spots for disease and insects. The latest research shows that the trunk wound doesn't have to be cut into the often-recommended oval shape. Removing good bark just delays the healing. Don't remove pieces of bark from the wound; the bark helps to speed healing.

My tree has a flap of loose bark. Should I wrap it down?

Jim ❖ No, just remove it with a sharp knife. The branch or trunk will heal over in a couple of seasons. If you leave the flap, it will harbour insect and disease pests, and won't help your trunk heal any more quickly.

We're often asked whether to apply pruning paint or tar to wounds on trees. Although this was a very common practice years ago, it was actually found to inhibit proper healing. Professional growers occasionally use paint on some species, but more often than not they leave the tree to do the work alone.

Tree collars provide excellent protection against rodents and lawn mowers.

My tree has been damaged by a lawnmower. Is there anything I can do to prevent further damage?

Jim ❖ Yes. Create a thin circle of mulch around the tree base, held in by landscape edging. Don't mulch right up to the trunk, though, or you may injure it.

You could also place a loose collar (such as plastic pipe) around the trunk. You could even install mesh fencing around trunk; fencing also helps to protect young trees from rodents. Planting a flowerbed around the tree is a nice aesthetically pleasing solution.

Why does my tree trunk have long, vertical cracks in it?

Jim ❖ These cracks could be the result of wind damage or even lightning, but most cracks are caused by freezing and thawing. In late winter, temperatures on the sunny side of the trunk can go well above freezing and then plunge to well below freezing at night. This can damage the bark and the cambium layer below, resulting in the vertical crack. Screens to keep the sun off the trunk can reduce this problem.

Insects

What is Dutch elm disease?

Jim ❖ This disease is a fungus that attacks primarily the American elm. It is carried on a beetle that tunnels into the wood, and during the tunneling the fungus is introduced to the tree. Once the fungus is established, the elm begins to slowly die. Treatments to control this disease once it enters the tree are expensive and not always effective. The American elm has been wiped out in most regions of North America.

Is there a Dutch elm disease-resistant tree?

Lois ❖ Yes. An elm has been bred specifically to resist Dutch elm disease. It's called, very appropriately, 'Liberty.' Thanks to this tree, the majestic elm may soon return to prominence in areas where the American elm has been wiped out by Dutch elm disease.

Jim ❖ 'Discovery' elm is another DED-resistant variety.

My tree is covered with red spiders. They just hatched out today. What are they? They aren't spidermites.

Lois ❖ If the spiders are quite large and mobile, they won't hurt your tree. In fact, they'll likely feed on potential pests. Many species of spiders inhabit trees searching for prey, and there's no reason to discourage them. Sometimes in our concern for keeping trees and shrubs healthy, we deal overzealously with insects. They play an important part in nature and most are actually harmless to plants.

What is dormant oil, and when do I use it?

Jim ❖ Dormant oil suffocates insects and is sprayed on when plants are dormant. It's harmful to leaves, so you should use it in late fall after the leaves have dropped or in early spring before the leaves begin to emerge.

What is summer oil?

Jim ❖ Summer oil is a highly refined oil. It can be applied to certain plants during the summer to control insect and disease pests. Summer oil is low in sulfonated compounds, which can harm plants; dormant oils, which are high in sulfonated compounds, can severely damage leafed-out plants. Even though summer oils are used during the summer, they can still injure many sensitive plants. Always read the label before applying.

Evaluating Hazardous Trees

Fall is an excellent time to evaluate potentially hazardous trees. The lack of leaves makes tree structures easier to examine, and the slower pace of fall gardening leaves more time for this important job. It takes a professional arborist to evaluate a tree thoroughly, but gardeners can do a lot to prevent tree accidents.

Here are a few tips for evaluating potentially hazardous trees. If you suspect a tree may be weak or unsafe, ask a certified arborist to inspect it.

• Look for signs of decay, including cavities (especially at the trunk), sap bleeding through bark, mushrooms, pests (ants, beehives), or loose bark.

poor pruning cut

• Trees with a pyramidal habit (evergreens, for example) should have a single trunk that extends from the ground to the growing tip. Pyramidal trees with forked trunks may split. For maximum stability, trees that form canopies should have several thick, evenly spaced branches (called scaffold branches) that spiral up the trunk.

deer damage

• Naturally leaning trees are not necessarily hazardous, but under certain conditions they may become so. Heavy loads of snow and ice, or even robust growth at the end of the tree, may prove too much to bear.

• Trees should have a "basal flare" at ground level-that is, the trunk should spread out as it enters the ground. If the trunk looks like a telephone pole stuck straight into the ground, the tree might suffer root failure and topple over.

• Improperly pruned trees are much more prone to failure than properly pruned trees. Take the time to learn correct pruning techniques, or get a certified arborist to prune your trees for you.

• Broken or dead branches are certain to fall sooner or later. Prune and dispose of broken and dead branches promptly.

My tree is covered in black, powdery film. What is it and will it kill my tree?

Lois ❖ What you're describing is not an insect, but it is most likely caused by one. Those black patches are sooty mould, which is growing on the honeydew excreted by aphids. Neither will kill your tree.

Aphids on a tree can best be controlled by spraying with a strong stream of water every few days for a few weeks. The sooty mould will clear up once the aphids are gone.

There are caterpillars all over the tree on my boulevard. Will they kill it?

Lois ❖ To answer this question properly I'd need a description of the caterpillar. If possible, take a sample caterpillar to your local garden centre for identification.

Severe caterpillar infestations can completely strip a tree of its leaves, and consecutive infestations can weaken the tree, leaving it vulnerable to other problems.

Jim ❖ Once you have identified the caterpillar, you can choose the control method that best works. Generally speaking, egg bands on branches can be removed by hand in the spring before the leaves emerge, and the caterpillar itself can be removed or treated by your city's parks and maintenance department.

I've been hearing a lot about satin moth. What's the concern?

Lois ❖ Satin moth caterpillars can be destructive, completely defoliating poplar and willow species; they will also eat leaves of other species if they are hungry enough. Trees will often recover, sending out new but smaller leaves. Years of consecutive infestations will weaken a tree, making it more susceptible to other insects and disease.

Jim ❖ Satin moth overwinters very successfully in cold climates. The larvae begin feeding in late May, consuming whole leaves and stripping entire trees. You'll notice most of the damage in mid June. The larvae are grey-brown with dark heads and pale-yellow patches on the back. Larvae moult and cast skins that are visible on the underside of branches. They cocoon in rolled leaves on twigs and in bark crevices. If you suspect you have an infestation but it's too late in the season to see larvae feeding actively, the presence of rolled leaves, larval skins, and silken webbing on branches should confirm your suspicions.

Adult moths emerge in July. They are satin-white with black bodies. Females lay clusters of light-green eggs on leaves, branches, or trunks. The eggs hatch in two weeks, and young larvae begin skeletonizing leaves. They then seek out spots to hibernate over winter. The satin moth's natural enemies include parasitic wasps, flies, mites, beetles, birds, and a virus. To control the moths, you can apply sprays to small outbreaks in spring once leaves are fully developed or in early to mid August when the young larvae are feeding.

The needles on my spruce trees appear to have been chewed by a dark-brown worm with a black head. What is it and how do I get rid of it?

Lois ❖ You are describing a spruce budworm or sawfly. These little worms are voracious feeders that can completely strip a tree of its new growth.

Jim ❖ To control this pest, you can hand pick (if the tree is small) or treat with an application of Latox in early to mid May, when new growth is beginning to show.

Year after year, the new leaves on my dogwood curl up. How do I treat it?

Lois ❖ It sounds like you have a recurring infestation of aphids. Chemical control is only necessary if the infestation is severe.

Jim ❖ There are a large number of aphid species that attack a wide variety of trees. Most species of aphids feed on the new leaves, causing distorted growth. Insecticidal soap, applied to the undersides of the leaves before the aphids become firmly established, can reduce the problem.

My white spruce has pink, almost cone-like tips. I'm sure they're not new cones. What are they?

Jim ❖ Your spruce most likely has cooley spruce gall adelgid. This pest first appears as cottony white specks in early spring. The nymphs overwinter and develop into females that reproduce without mating, depositing eggs that hatch and draw sap from the new growth. The adelgid causes the branch tips to swell and grow around the invaders, yielding the cone-like galls you describe. Pruning off and destroying the galls as soon as you see them will reduce the adult population, and applying appropriate insecticide in early spring will kill the juveniles.

Animals

A rabbit has eaten the bark of my two-year-old apple tree. What can I do?

Jim ❖ It's difficult to repair a trunk injured by rodent feeding. If the damage is limited to a small area, the tree will heal over time. If the damage is more extensive, it must be bridge-grafted. Bridge-grafting involves taking several finger-thick branches, bridging across the damaged area and inserting each end into the cambium of the tree trunk; this treatment requires a lot of knowledge and skill, so you might want to consult a certified arborist.

You can try to prevent further rodent damage by applying a protective collar around the base of the trunk.

Is there any way to keep cats away from my shrubs? They seem to like my kiwi plants in particular.

Lois ❖ One of our staff has had great success using a perennial plant called *Salvia nemerosa* (especially 'May Night') in her shrub beds. She says that her cats won't go near the stuff!

Jim ❖ No product is completely effective at repelling cats, but there are several worth trying:

- Cat and dog repellents
- Hot-pepper repellents
- Fencing and barriers
- Pinecones
- Motion-activated water sprinkler.

CHAPTER 7 ❦
TREE AND SHRUB VARIETIES

*Different species of trees and shrubs
naturally require specific treatment, and
even different varieties within a single
species can require vastly different care.
When choosing varieties, make sure to look
beyond aesthetic benchmarks like growth
habit and colour. Check out cold hardiness
and care requirements, too. Just because one
variety of weigela or forsythia is hardy for
your region doesn't mean that another
variety is equally tough.*

Apple

I've heard about a blight that affects apple trees, and I'm a little worried. Can you tell me more?

Lois ❖ You're thinking of fireblight. Keeping fireblight at bay requires constant vigilance.

Jim ❖ Fireblight is caused by a bacteria called *Cerwinia caratovora. Caratovora* is Latin for "starch eater." It's a good name, since fireblight breaks down the starches in tree shoots, flowers, and leaves. Some apples are more resistant to fireblight than others; check with your local nursery for the most resistant varieties. Avoid excessive application of high-nitrogen fertilizers that cause soft, leafy growth, which is more prone to fireblight attack. Pruning as soon as a branch becomes infected is your best control strategy; prune at least 15 cm below the visibly affected area.

What causes scab on apple, and how can I prevent it?

Jim ❖ This is a fungal disease called *Venturia inaequalis*. It attacks leaves and blossoms as well as fruit, but people usually first notice it on the fruit.

The disease overwinters on fallen leaves, so it's particularly critical to clean up your apple leaves in the fall. The problem tends to be worst during periods of high humidity and cool temperatures (16–24°C). The severity of the infection drops substantially at tempertures above 26°C.

'Harcourt' apple

My apple tree bloomed in the spring and now it's blooming again in late summer. Why?

Lois ❖ Severely pruned apple trees often rebloom.

Jim ❖ Severe pruning causes a hormonal imbalance that triggers flowering. The tree is not harmed by late flowering, but always try to follow good pruning practices to prevent this problem.

Ash

How far apart should I space green ash trees?

Jim ❖ Space them about 4 m apart if you want them to act as a wind barrier. If you're planting them individually, space them at least twice that far apart for good symmetry. Green ash has a large canopy, which is why ash trees are too large for many yards.

Azalea

Which azaleas are hardiest?

Lois ❖ The 'Northern Light' series is very tough and produces spectacular colour in the spring. However, within the series some varieties—such as 'Lemon Lights'—are more prone to winter-kill.

Jim ❖ If you lose a 'Northern Light' azalea to winter-kill, it may need more-acidic soil. Your plants will weaken over time unless the soil pH is between 5.0 and 5.5. Acidify your soil before planting and use an acid fertilizer like 30-10-10 regularly.

Why are my azaleas all veiny?

Lois ❖ When azaleas develop leaves with very prominent veins, that usually means there's a nutrient deficiency. Try some 30-10-10 fertilizer.

Jim ❖ The veininess is due to an iron deficiency. Either the soil is deficient in iron or it's very alkaline, preventing the roots from drawing up the iron. Azaleas like acidic soils with a pH of 6.0 or lower and lots of iron. Get a soil test to determine your soil's pH level.

'Golden Lights' azalea

I pruned my azaleas and now I don't have any flowers. Why?

Jim ❖ You may have pruned your azaleas improperly. Azalea flower buds grow and mature during the summer, blooming the following spring. If the azaleas are heavily pruned or sheared, the flower buds will be removed along with the branches. It will take a full year for the flowers to come back.

If you pruned carefully to avoid chopping off flower buds and still don't have any flowers the following year, it's possible that a severe winter killed the buds.

How can I tell the difference between a rhododendron and an azalea?

Lois ❖ True rhododendrons have ten or more stamens. Their leaves are scaly and have small reddish dots on the undersurfaces. Azaleas have five stamens and their leaves are never dotted with scales. New hybrids, however, can have five to ten stamens.

Birch

Why has the top of my birch tree died?

Jim ❖ There are several possible explanations:

- It may be suffering from moisture stress. Birch trees grow best in moist, cool soil. Hot, dry soil damages the roots. Always keep birch moist, particularly during hot spells.
- Your tree could be growing on a dry slope.
- You may have a bug problem. The bronze birch borer attacks the tops of birch trees.

• Yellow-bellied sapsuckers often damage birch trees. Their presence is indicated by a series of small holes along the trunk.

When should I prune birch trees?

Lois ❖ Birch doesn't normally require much pruning because it has a nice, natural open form. If you must prune, it's best to do so shortly after the tree comes into full leaf. If you prune earlier, the tree loses a lot of sap from the cut ends of the branches. This doesn't cause any long-term harm, but it is unsightly.

Jim ❖ Be sure to wash the tree off when the sap stops flowing to avoid attracting pests. With birch, always aim to prune a little each year rather than a lot every few years.

What made the holes in my birch tree?

Jim ❖ If you find regularly spaced holes in rows, your tree has been visited by the yellow-bellied sapsucker. This bird bores regular rows of holes in the upper portion of the tree trunk to feed on the sugary sap.

Some people deter sapsuckers by hanging wind chimes or aluminum pie plates in the tree. If you don't mind the aesthetics and you're not trying to attract birds to your yard, this can be a good solution.

Which pest poses the most serious threat to birch trees?

Jim ❖ Birch leaf miner is a serious pest, particularly from an aesthetic point of view. The leaves attacked by the birch leaf miner turn brown quickly as the insect tunnels and feeds within the leaves. Systemic insecticides containing dimethoate have proven quite effective in controlling leaf miner. Timing, however, is critical; follow the manufacturer's instructions.

Parasitic wasps, a biological control for birch leaf miner, have recently been introduced into various North American regions with good success. Thanks to them, the use of dimethoate is diminishing. If these beneficial insects have been introduced in your region, avoid dimethoate so as not to injure them.

What are the horizontal lines on birch bark?

Jim ❖ These lines are called lenticels. They are important for gas exchange, allowing gases produced by the birch tree to exit into the atmosphere.

Buffaloberry

I've heard that buffaloberry doesn't need fertilizer. Can this be true?

Jim ❖ Well, it's partly true. Buffaloberry has the ability to fix nitrogen in the soil. In other words, the plant's roots, in conjunction with nitrogen-fixing bacteria, can convert gaseous nitrogen in the soil into a form that the plant can use. Therefore, nitrogen fertilizers are unnecessary. However, buffaloberry benefits from the addition of phosphorus and potassium to the soil.

Cedar

Can I cut off the top of my cedar?

Jim ❖ People often consider topping (cutting the top off) a cedar if it's growing into an eavestrough or overhead power line. Unfortunately, this will cause the tree to become bushy at the cuts and will lessen its aesthetic appeal.

Lois ❖ Short of removing the cedar, all you can do is to keep it well trimmed. When choosing a cedar for a confined location, pick one of the shorter varieties. They have all the same characteristics as the larger ones, except the height.

Why do my cedars turn brown in the spring?

Lois ❖ The simplest answer is that they dry out over the winter. Anyone who grows cedars in regions with rapidly fluctuating late-winter temperatures has probably experienced this problem.

Jim ❖ The worst time for cedars is the early spring, when bright, warm, windy days are followed by much cooler days. Since the ground is often still frozen, the cedars cannot replace the moisture lost through the needles. A thorough watering in the fall helps, as do wind screens that keep sun and wind off the foliage, reducing moisture loss. Antidessicant spray helps, too. Older cedars suffer less than younger cedars, since their roots are better established.

Which cedar suffers least from winter browning?

Jim ❖ The healthiest ones suffer the least, provided the variety is hardy for your area. We've had very little browning on 'Brandon,' 'Rushmore,' 'Techny,' 'Holmstrup,' and 'Wareana' cedars.

'Little Giant' cedar

Choose a healthy cedar, prepare the soil carefully, keep it well watered, and you shouldn't see much winter browning. The critical period is the first two years after transplanting. Established cedars suffer less from browning.

What fertilizer should I use on my cedars?

Lois ❖ I have consistent results with 30-10-10. Don't forget, though, that frequent watering is more important than fertilizer.

Jim ❖ A soil test helps to determine what, if any, fertilizer you should add to the soil. However, 30-10-10 is excellent in most situations. Just remember that more is not better. To avoid burning your plants, always apply the amount recommended on the label.

My cedars are turning black on the bottom branches. What's the problem?

Lois ❖ Dog urine is the most likely culprit. Dog urine contains high levels of salt, which can burn foliage, turning it black. If possible, wash down the affected area immediately after the dog urinates. Then do your best to keep the dog away from the tree in the future. You may have to put up a barrier.

Jim ❖ We once had a customer who swore that window-washing spray caused the same blackening on the top of his cedar. Both urine and many cleaning solutions contain ammonia, so that may be possible.

What are the brown things at the top of my cedar?

Lois ❖ Those are cones. Cedars are coniferous trees, meaning that they produce seed-bearing cones, much like spruce and pine. Cedar cones open in autumn and release their seeds during the winter.

Can I grow large cedars in half barrels and overwinter them in my garage?

Jim ❖ Probably not. Your biggest challenge will be trying to keep them from getting too warm or too cold. If the temperature rises just a few degrees above freezing, the cedars will begin to grow. Without adequate light, they will quickly burn up their energy resources and die. The cedars can also be easily damaged if the temperature drops too low. Most garages simply aren't designed to provide the environment your cedars need.

Cherry

Why are my Nanking cherries veiny?

Lois ❖ It sounds like you're growing them in alkaline soil. Get a soil test to be sure, and do not add lime to the soil.

Jim ❖ Veiny leaves on the upper part of the plant are typically caused by iron deficiency. As Mom says, watch the lime. Lime makes a soil more alkaline, and alkaline soils prevent the roots from taking up iron from the soil.

'Danica' cedar

Why don't my cherry trees produce fruit?

Lois ❖ I can see two possibilities: either the trees are too young or you have a pollination problem.

Jim ❖ Most cherry trees require cross-pollination for fruiting. Choose varieties that will cross-pollinate to ensure success, and keep in mind that the two trees must bloom at the same time.

As Mom suggests, your trees may still be too immature to produce fruit. Bitter winter cold or late-spring frosts may have damaged flowerbuds or flowers, destroying any chance of fruit. In that case, all you can do is hope for better luck next season.

How can I tell whether I have a double-flowering plum or Nanking cherry?

Jim ❖ When they're not in bloom, these trees appear nearly identical. But if the foliage is fuzzy, it's a Nanking cherry, hence the Latin name *Prunus tomentosa*, meaning "hairy."

Cork

Is it true that there are male and female cork trees?

Jim ❖ Yes. We don't often see plants as male and female, but they do exist. Cork trees are dioecious, meaning that male and female flowers are produced on separate trees. Tree propagators often grow only male clones to avoid the problem of seed production and fruit fall from female trees.

Cotoneaster

My cotoneaster hedge has white stuff on the stems. What is it?

Jim ❖ The likely cause is an insect called scale. Scale loves hedges that have become weak and overgrown. Spray dormant oil in the late fall or very early spring (just as the leaf buds are swelling), and remove old wood.

What are those raised orange spots on the branches of my cotoneaster ?

Jim ❖ *Nectria* or *Cytospora* are fungi that attack dead or dying wood on many species of trees and shrubs. No effective chemical control has been found, and control is really not necessary as the wood the fungi attack should be pruned out anyway.

What is the best way to prune cotoneasters?

Lois ❖ Cotoneasters should always taper from the bottom up, not the top down. That means the top should be narrower than the bottom to allow light to reach the lower growth. If the light doesn't reach the bottom, branches will thin out. Tapering also prevents a heavy snow from splitting a hedge.

Jim ❖ Don't forget to prune out old wood on a regular basis to keep the plant vigorous and to reduce scurfy scale.

We have found that the average lifespan of a healthy-looking hedge is 20 to 25 years. Hedges can be rejuvenated by cutting them down to 15 cm (when they are dormant). In two or three years, the hedge will be bushy and 60 cm in size.

cotoneaster hedge

'Kelsey' crabapple

Crabapple

Do crabapples come in a variety of colours?

Lois. Yes. Crabapple flowers can appear in a wide range of hues of white, red, and pink. I particularly love ornamental crabapples, which produce some of the finest spring flower shows.

Cranberry

Do cranberry bushes produce the fruit we buy for turkey dressing?

Lois ❖ No. What we call a cranberry bush is actually a member of the genus *Viburnum*, while store-bought cranberries come from bushes of the *Vaccinium* genus, which also includes blueberries. Garden cranberry bushes produce rich, tart red berries that somewhat resemble the cranberries you buy at the grocery store.

Which cranberry has good fall colour?

Lois ❖ Cranberries are hardy, undemanding shrubs that work very well in the urban landscape, and their fall colour is an exciting way to extend their seasonal interest. 'Alfredo,' 'American Highbush,' 'Bailey's Compact,' and 'Wentworth' are all excellent choices for fall colour ranging from yellow to red.

Can cranberries tolerate shade?

Lois ❖ Cranberries are one of the best shrubs for shady areas. Don't get me wrong: cranberries do love sun, and the more they get, the better. But they can tolerate a degree of shade.

Currant

What's the white stuff on my currants?

Jim ❖ Currants are prone to attack by a fungal disease called powdery mildew. It looks like white powder and appears on the upper surface of the leaves. Powdery mildew is particularly bad when the days are hot and dry and the nights are cool. These conditions allow a film of dew to form on the foliage. Powdery mildew spores germinate in this layer of moisture and infect the leaves. If you've had a history of problems with powdery mildew, treat the foliage with fungicide once the shrub is fully leafed out.

What are the worms that are attacking my currants?

Lois ❖ Currant worms are actually the larval stage of the sawfly, a tiny, wasp-like insect. They have a voracious appetite, and a currant bush can be devoured in a couple of days by currant worms. Currant worms tend to blend in with the foliage, so you have to be on the lookout for these pests. Brushing the currant with your hand to dislodge the pests and crushing the worms is an effective way to control them.

Jim ❖ The fly lays its eggs at the base of the flower. When the egg hatches, the maggot burrows into the newly forming fruit and matures as the fruit matures. The maggot leaves a tunnel and exit hole in every fruit it attacks. Upon exiting the fruit, the maggot falls to the ground and pupates to an adult.

To control currant worms, you can also spray with diazonon or fruit-tree spray just as the flowers are finishing, then again in 10–12 days.

Can currants be used as hedge plants?

Lois ❖ Yes. The alpine currant in particular makes an excellent hedge.

Daphne

Why does my daphne die over the winter?

Lois ❖ Exposure to cold, dry winds can kill these shrubs. Plant daphne in a sheltered area and mulch every fall to protect the flowerbuds during the winter. Daphne also benefits from the insulation of snow cover.

Elder

How do I keep my elder foliage from turning black?

Lois ❖ Plant it in a location where the ground is cool and moist.

Jim ❖ Elder produces abundant green growth, which requires lots of water; the foliage turns black when the plant has insufficient moisture, such as in hot, dry locations. A shallow layer of mulch will help keep the soil moist.

Elderberry

Can elderberries be eaten?

Lois ❖ Yes, elderberries can be used for wine, jellies, and ice cream.

Elm

Why did my elms develop long, finger-like projections on their leaves?

Jim ❖ These strange-looking growths are caused by mites. When the mites feed on the leaves, they secrete chemicals that mimic plant hormones, causing the leaves to envelop them. The mites cause no long-term harm to the elm, so don't worry about trying to control them.

Fir

What is the difference between fir and spruce?

Lois ❖ Firs and spruce are both evergreens and conifers, but they belong to different genera. Firs can be distinguished from spruce by their flat needles; spruces have sharp, round needles.

rose daphne

Forsythia

Why didn't my forsythia bloom this spring?

Jim ❖ Forsythia flowerbuds can die during a cold winter. The leaf buds are tougher and will usually survive. Plant forsythia in a sheltered area and mulch every fall to protect the flowerbuds during the winter.

Genista

Can I plant genista in my rock garden?

Lois ❖ Certainly. This shrub likes well-drained soils and full sun, and puts on a brilliant display of golden flowers. It makes a great groundcover for hot, dry rock gardens.

Can I collect seeds from my 'Vancouver Gold' genista?

Jim ❖ You can, but there's no use planting them. The 'Vancouver Gold' variety is sterile and won't produce viable seeds.

'Lydia' genista

Gingko

I've heard that a prehistoric tree still grows today. What is it?

Jim ❖ Gingko trees have been around for 150 million years, providing shade for dinosaurs, humans, and everything that lived in-between. Gingko makes a great feature tree, with its unusual leaves, but it's very slow-growing and requires a sheltered spot.

What is the tree that people sometimes use to increase their memory?

Lois ❖ That would be the gingko biloba tree. The leaves are often harvested for inclusion in herbal memory supplements.

Jim ❖ Not all ginkgoes are created equal; the age of the leaves and the storage conditions have a great effect on quality. When using herbal supplements, consult with a physician to make sure you're getting the right product to suit your needs.

Hawthorn

The hawthorn planted in my yard has suckers coming from the base. Can I prune them off and stop them from coming back?

Lois ❖ The shoots you see coming from the base are actually not suckers but watersprouts. You can prune them off as they appear. Healthy trees that are well maintained tend not to produce watersprouts.

Hazelnut

Can I grow hazelnuts and harvest them in my own yard?

Lois ❖ You certainly can grow and harvest this nut-bearing shrub in your yard—if you have the space! Hazelnuts spread easily and somewhat aggressively, forming dense thickets. In the home garden, thin hazelnut by pruning annually in late winter and removing basal shoots as they appear. You'll know the nuts are ready to harvest when the skin over them begins to brown and curl. Enjoy them raw or baked.

Holly

Why does my holly dry out over the winter?

Jim ❖ Holly normally retains its glossy foliage over winter, but during long, cold winters the foliage can dry out. Mulch and snow cover help to preserve the foliage, although that will block your view of the leaves. In mild, coastal regions, holly doesn't require mulching.

Hydrangea

Can we grow hydrangea in cooler climates?

Lois ❖ Yes, provided you choose from among the hardy varieties; 'PeeGee' is a good choice. Check with your local garden centre.

When should I prune hydrangea? I think mine is coming back from the ground and the top seems to die back each year.

Lois ❖ When to prune hydrangea depends on the variety and your climate zone. For example, 'PeeGee' hydrangea won't die back to the ground in zone 5, but it may very well in zone 2. Prune off any dead or winter-killed wood in spring and selectively prune out old wood as needed.

'Annabelle' hydrangea

Juniper

My juniper has raised, jelly-like bumps shaped like starfish. What's causing this, and how do I treat it?

Jim ❖ *Gymnosporangium juniperi-virginianae,* or cedar-apple rust, is a fungal disease with a spectacular, almost alien appearance. It has an interacting life cycle, which means that it requires two hosts to complete its life cycle. It causes yellowish orange leaf spots on apple and galls that produce jelly-like horns on cedar and juniper. To treat, spray the apple tree with a product that contains ferbam as its active ingredient twice during the flowerbud stage (wait 10–14 days between applications) and spray the juniper in late summer or early fall.

If you see those odd jelly stars on your juniper, pinch them off and be thorough in your fall clean-up of leaves and fruit around the affected apple trees.

My juniper is old and overgrown, and it looks awful. What can I do with it? If I cut it back, will it bush out?

Lois ❖ I'm afraid not. Most evergreens simply will not fill out if you prune them back. Instead of cutting your juniper back, try pruning it to a different shape or form. For example, I've seen an old juniper pruned to a bonsai form—very striking!

Jim ❖ Sometimes it's best to bite the bullet and replace an old plant with a smaller variety that fits your space and can be properly maintained from the start.

Lilac

Why isn't my lilac blooming? What can I do?

Lois ❖ If lilac is immature or growing in a spot with too much shade, it will not bloom. Perhaps the flower buds were removed in a bout of over-enthusiastic pruning. Lilac flowers can be pruned after they turn brown, but don't cut back too hard; otherwise, you could remove the buds for the next season's blooms.

Jim ❖ Lilacs need a minimum of six hours of direct sunlight each day to set flowerbuds. Over-fertilizing with nitrogen can also prevent blooming. Prune lilacs only after the flowers fade. Otherwise, you may inadvertently cut off next year's flowerbuds. Severe pruning at any time of year will disrupt blooming.

It's early spring, and my lilac is partially blocking my driveway. Can I prune it now?

Jim ❖ Go right ahead. You'll be removing some of this year's flowerbuds, but you won't harm the plant.

How many colours of lilacs are there?

Lois ❖ Lilacs come in seven official colours. John Wister of Pennsylvania, an author, scholar, and horticulturist, classified lilacs by colour in 1941. His official colours are white, violet, blue, lavender, pink, magenta, and purple.

Grow a Lilac!

Lilacs are wonderful in shrub beds, screens, hedges, or as a showy specimen plant. Their remarkable look and fragrance improve any yard. They should be grown in sun to light shade; ideally, they should receive full sun for two-thirds of the day for the best show of flowers. They must not be planted in wet, boggy soil. Lilacs need excellent drainage to avoid drowning; sandy, gravelly loam is best. Plant them well away from competing trees and shrubs.

Pruning is critical to the long-term health and beauty of lilacs. Don't postpone pruning; do it once a year, faithfully. Every year, prune out any wild, thin suckers, any declining stems, all twiggy small branches, and a quarter to a third of the older branches and suckers. Pruning will prolong the life of your lilac and will keep it looking fresh and new. Never shear a lilac! Once the flowers have faded, remove them, but don't cut too far down; otherwise, you'll sever the dormant flowerbuds, which means you'll see no flowers next year.

Maackia

I want to plant a maackia in my front yard. What type of soil does it prefer?

Lois ❖ Amur maackia is a great choice for a front yard. It thrives in average garden soil. This member of the legume family is compact and tidy, rarely needs pruning, and has attractive, sweet-smelling blooms in midsummer.

Maple

What causes the round lumps on maple leaves?

Jim ❖ Very tiny mites called eriophyid mites cause all sorts of weird growths on maple foliage. They secrete a substance that causes the leaves to swell and encapsulate them.

Once the lumps and bumps appear, there's almost no way to control them. If you've had severe infestations in the past, begin treatment at the tight-bud stage, in the spring. Spray the tree with dormant oil or a miticide. Repeated severe infestations can weaken a tree and contribute to its death. Fortunately, apart from the cosmetic damage, the mites don't cause any significant harm in a single season.

My maple is quite sparse and generally looks very poor. It is planted in full sun in good soil on a steep slope in my yard. What's wrong with it?

Lois ❖ Although you don't state specifically what kind of maple you're growing, I would suspect that the problem may be moisture related. Many maples prefer well-drained soil, but they like to be on the moist side. Your slope may be steep enough that the maple is getting insufficient water. Water the soil directly under the tree to see how quickly it runs off.

Why are maples more intensely coloured some years than others?

Jim ❖ Maple colours depend on species and weather. The sugar maple produces intense red leaves, while the Manitoba maple produces mostly yellow leaves.

Bright, warm late-summer days with cool nights produce the best fall display, because this kind of weather increases the production of anthocyanins, the leaf pigments that are responsible for red foliage.

Can you harvest maple syrup from trees other than the sugar maple?

Jim ❖ Yes, the Manitoba maple yields a sugary sap much like the sugar maple. You can also harvest birch trees for sugar. Birches have about one percent sugar in their sap, along with minerals like calcium and potassium. But if you're planning to tap the trees in your garden, be warned: it takes about 40 L of sap to make 1 L of syrup.

mayday tree

Mayday

My mayday tree has lots of small holes in the leaves. What are they?

Jim ❖ These could be due to several causes, but the most likely culprit is a fungal disease called shothole. You will probably notice that the tree recovers on its own; very rarely is there lasting damage. We see often shothole on Schubert chokecherry and purpleleaf sandcherry.

There are black, nut-like clusters on my mayday. What are they and how do I cure them?

Jim ❖ Your tree has likely been stricken with a serious plant disease called black knot of cherry. At the fruiting stage, the disease seems to billow out of the branch or trunk. The only solution is to prune out the affected branches well below the knot. Be sure to seal the pruned branches in a plastic garbage bag and to clean your pruning tools between cuts with a bleach or ethyl alcohol solution to prevent spreading this disease. It affects all members of the genus *Prunus*—cherry, mayday, plum, etc.

How do I stop maydays from suckering?

Lois ❖ This is an inherent trait of the mayday, and only careful, regular pruning will control the suckers.

Jim ❖ In fact, excessive pruning and stress can increase sucker production. Prune off suckers as they appear and keep the mayday well watered. Fertilizer may also reduce stress.

Mock orange

Why is a mock orange called a mock orange?

Lois ❖ If you ever walk by a mock orange in full flower on a warm summer day, you'll immediately understand why it's been given this name. The flowers have a delicate orange scent that I just adore.

Jim ❖ The scent is the only trait that relates the mock orange to the citrus tree: they're entirely different species. Many people call mock orange the jasmine tree because of its fragrance.

Mountain ash

I have black soot on the branches of my mountain ash. What is it?

Jim ✤ It's likely a fungal disease called sooty mould. The mould does not harm the tree but grows on the sticky sap secreted by aphids. In other words, if you have sooty mould, aphids are feeding on your tree. Eliminate them and you eliminate the problem.

I want to plant a mountain ash but my yard is quite small. Can I just keep it pruned to size?

Lois ✤ Well, you could keep pruning but that's an awful lot of work and you may end up with a very distorted form. Instead, why not plant a smaller variety such as 'Columnar' or 'Peking'? If those don't appeal to you, consider a different species altogether that will give you a similar appearance but require a smaller area.

What is a good dwarf mountain ash?

Jim ✤ One of the best small mountain ash varieties is the showy mountain ash. It reaches only about 4.5 m in height and has a very attractive, dense, compact growth habit.

Oak

I am going to plant an oak to commemorate the birth of my granddaughter. Can you recommend a fast-growing oak?

Lois ✤ I call this heritage planting: planting for the enjoyment of future generations. What a great way to celebrate a wonderful occasion! Oak is a good choice as it is extremely long lived. Different varieties grow at different rates, and growth also depends on your zone. One of the faster-growing oaks is the pin oak; northern red oak also grows comparatively quickly.

What are those funny bumps on my oak leaves?

Jim ❖ These are produced by an insect pest called the gall wasp. There are several species of gall wasp, but they all produce strange swellings on any oak leaves they touch. The insects don't cause any long-term damage to the oak, but the swellings can be rather unsightly.

red oak

Pine

How and when should I prune my mugo pine?

Lois ❖ This is a quick, easy task. Simply break off about a third of each of the candles in the spring to keep the mugo stocky and dense. You can use secateurs, but I find that it's quicker and easier to snap the candles off with my fingers.

Can I mound the soil around the base of my mugo pine?

Jim ❖ A little bit of mounding won't hurt, but a thick layer of soil around the base can suffocate the roots. Don't mound the soil right up against the trunk.

In the fall, the inside needles on my pine turn yellow and drop off. What's the problem? Can I correct it?

Lois ❖ This is natural and nothing to worry about. Like deciduous trees, evergreens shed leaves in the fall. Unlike deciduous leaves, however, the needles last for several seasons before dropping off. Some years you may see more drop than others, which may be related to summer drought conditions.

I've heard that a pine is the oldest living plant on Earth. Is this true?

Jim ❖ A 5,000-year-old bristlecone pine growing in the White Mountains of California is certainly one of the oldest living things on the planet. But 20 years ago scientists discovered a creosote bush in the Mojave desert that they estimate is 12,000 years old.

columnar Scotch pine

What's this yellow dust on my pine tree? Help!

Jim ❖ Don't panic; it's just pine pollen. In the spring, pollen cones burst open, releasing millions of tiny pollen grains that fertilize the seed cones. Pines have both male and female flowers; the hard cones are the female structures, while the soft, brown cones are male.

What is the difference between soft pines and hard pines?

Jim ❖ Soft pines, including western white, bristlecone, and eastern white, have bundles of five needles, smooth twigs, and no prickles on the cone scales. Hard pines, such as the lodgepole, red, and ponderosa, have bundles of two or three needles, ridged twigs, and prickled cones.

Potentilla

Can I divide potentillas?

Lois ❖ Not easily. You would be more successful taking cuttings. Unlike perennials, woody shrubs don't divide well.

Rhododendron

Can I grow rhododendrons in a cooler climate?

Jim ❖ Yes. Plant breeders have developed some outstanding varieties that are both beautiful and tough. The buds of the Finnish rhododendron, for example, can tolerate temperatures of −35°C. All rhododendrons perform best in acidic soil, in a site that collects snow and is protected from winter wind.

'Cloudland' rhododendron

Spruce

How can I kill the bugs that are attacking the top of my spruce tree?

Jim ❖ The white pine weevil, a fairly common pest of spruce and pine, prefers to attack new, succulent top growth. Adult weevils attack the evergreen in early spring, boring holes in the leader and laying eggs.

Chemical control in the early spring will prevent an attack, but once weevils have bored in you must cut off the leader below the damage. Slice it open and look for the end of the bored tunnel to ensure you've cut far enough.

Why do blue spruce vary in colour intensity?

Lois ❖ The colour intensity depends largely on the variety and the soil. If you want an intense blue colour, choose a variety with a strong genetic trait for blue needles such as 'Hoopsi,' R.H. Montgomery,' or 'Fat Albert.'

Jim ❖ If a blue spruce fades over the years, it's likely not getting enough iron, a critical nutrient for blue colouration. The soil itself could be iron deficient, or it could be too alkaline to allow the plant to easily absorb the iron. A soil test can tell you if alkalinity is the problem, in which case you can take steps to acidify the soil. If iron levels are low, apply chelated iron or an iron-enhanced evergreen fertilizer.

'Little Gem' spruce

Why won't anything grow under my spruce trees?

Jim ❖ There's a combination of reasons. Spruce provides heavy shade, blocking sunlight from the soil below. The roots draw vast amounts of water, leaving the surface soil dry. The needles act as a natural mulch, blocking growth, and they're allelopathic, meaning that they release chemicals that inhibit the growth of other plants. The needles are also slightly acidic, which can affect the pH of the soil over many years.

'Fat Albert' spruce

black walnut

Walnut

I've heard that nothing should be planted near a black walnut. Why?

Jim ❖ Black walnut exudes a chemical called juglone from its roots. This chemical acts as a protective herbicide, inhibiting the growth of plants that try to compete with the walnut for resources like water, nutrients, and light. Tomatoes can be severely injured by juglone; most other plants are less susceptible to damage from this chemical.

Of course, planting tomatoes around the base of a black walnut is a recipe for disaster, juglone or not. Walnuts cast long, dark shadows that prevent almost anything from growing.

Willow

My willow branches are turning black. They start to leaf out, then they shrivel and turn black. Why?

Jim ❖ This sounds like a leaf blight caused by bacteria or fungi. Diseases are more of a problem during rainy spells. Fortunately, these types of blights usually don't pose any long-term threat. Don't bother spraying; just let the disease run its course. We commonly see these blights on dogwoods as well.

I've heard that chewing willow bark will relieve headaches. Is this true?

Jim ❖ There is probably some truth in this. The genus name of willow is *Salix*, which is related to salicylic acid, a chemical found in willows. Aspirin tablets contain acetylsalicylic acid, a common pain reliever.

Incidentally, spirea also contains a fair bit of salicylic acid. But the concentrations in trees are relatively low, so rather than chewing bark I'd simply take an aspirin.

Afterword

by Jim Hole

I love to learn. I guess that's why I've always been more interested in the mechanics of the real world than the imaginary narratives of novels or films. Don't get me wrong: I love a good story as much as the next guy, but a chance to learn about the inner workings of nature holds more appeal for me. Sometimes Mom describes me as a kind of walking gardening encyclopedia, but the truth is, as you might have guessed, a little more complex. And although my sister-in-law calls me "Mr. Science," I don't pretend to know everything. But it bugs me if someone asks me a question and I don't know the answer. More often than not, the solution isn't in my head; I have to pull out a textbook or consult a specialist. Over the years I've naturally assimilated plenty of gardening knowledge because of that inability to let a question go without a response. Putting together these books has been very fulfilling for that reason; your questions gave me plenty of opportunity to do some extra research, and to discover a number of things I wasn't previously aware of.

Every year, trees and shrubs present a wide variety of new challenges and mysteries to science; indeed, that's one of the reasons that I find them so fascinating. But the grandeur and the history of these long-lived plants compels me even more. There's something humbling about knowing that the trees planted on Mom and Dad's farm long before I was born could still be around long after I'm gone. I can't help but be moved and even awed by such venerable strength and grace.

So Ask Us Some Questions...

We plan to update all of the *Question and Answer* books periodically. If you have a gardening question that's been troubling you, write to us! While we *can't* answer your inquiries individually, your question may appear in future Q&A books—along with the answer, naturally. And don't ever think that a question is "dumb" or "too simple." Odds are that any mysteries you face are shared by countless other gardeners.

Send your questions to:

Hole's Q&A Questions
101 Bellerose Drive
St. Albert, AB T8N 8N8
CANADA

You can also send us email at yourquestions@enjoygardening.com, or visit us at www.enjoygardening.com.

Index

Question: *Who is Lois Hole?*

Answer ❖ The author of eight best-selling books, Lois Hole provides practical advice that's both accessible and essential. Her knowledge springs from years of hands-on experience as a gardener and greenhouse operator. She's shared that knowledge for years through her books, her popular newspaper columns, hundreds of gardening talks all over the continent, and dozens of radio and television appearances. Never afraid to get her hands dirty, Lois answers all of your gardening questions with warmth and wit.

A member of the Order of Canada, Lois is the recipient of honorary degrees from Athabasca University and the University of Alberta, where she served as Chancellor from 1998-2000. She currently serves as Alberta's Lieutenant Governor.

Question: *Who is Jim Hole?*

Answer ❖ Inheriting his mother's love of horticulture, Jim Hole grew up in the garden. After spending his formative years on the Hole farm in St. Albert, Jim attended the University of Alberta, expanding his knowledge and earning a Bachelor of Science in Agriculture. Jim appears regularly on radio and television call-in shows to share what he's learned, and writes regular gardening columns for the *Edmonton Journal*, the *National Post*, the *Old Farmer's Almanac*, and the *Old Farmer's Almanac Gardener's Companion*. He has also contributed to *Canadian Gardening* magazine. Jim's focus is on the science behind the garden; he explains what makes plants tick in a clear and concise style, without losing sight of the beauty and wonder that makes gardening worthwhile.

Lois and Jim have worked together for years on books, newspaper articles, and gardening talks. With family members Ted Hole, Bill Hole, and Valerie Hole, Lois and Jim helped create Hole's, a greenhouse and garden centre that ranks among the largest retail gardening operations in Canada. The books in the *Q&A* series mark Lois and Jim's first official collaboration as authors.

One last question...

Was it hard to make this trees & shrubs book?

Yes. Although trees have always been a part of Hole's, the sheer breadth of information available for the thousands of varieties of trees and shrubs made this a difficult book to produce. To answer specific questions with such a broad scope of possible answers to draw from made the process difficult and at times nearly impossible.

As the questions were gathered and prepared we realized that this book could not be as encompassing as some of the others in the series and yet, at the same time, it was probably the most important volume. There are many simple, common sense rules about caring for trees and shrubs but they often get lost among the particular needs of the species and varieties. To give practical advice we always had to keep in mind the differences between a plant raised and sold by our nursery and the old bristlecone pine that has been in someone's yard for over 100 years.

More often than not, questions as simple as "what spruce is the bluest?" were most often answered with a less-than-definitive "It depends...." The answers in this book was very much a team effort. Earl Woods, Scott Rollans and Lois Hole and others combined their efforts to provide simple, easily understood advice, while Jim Hole, Shane Neufeld and Christina McDonald worked with the rest of the staff to create answers with depth and clarity. We had many discussions which often raised still more questions!

When the editorial and production staff joined the mix, they asked even more questions in helping to produce a text that could both introduce the vast world of arboriculture and provide great advice and practical information.

By the time the final proofs were done, more than a dozen experts from many different fields had added their own "practical advice and the science behind it" to make this book. More than any of the other books in this series, we believe this is more a volume of questions than a book of answers. We hope that you learned something new, were inspired to find out even more on your own, and are better prepared to nurture your own trees and shrubs.

Publication Management ❖ Bruce Timothy Keith
Series Editor ❖ Scott Rollans
Editor ❖ Leslie Vermeer
Editorial Assistant ❖ Christina McDonald
Writing & Editing ❖ Earl J. Woods
Book Design and Production ❖ Gregory Brown